THE
TESTAMENTS OF THE
TWELVE PATRIARCHS

BY

R. H. CHARLES, D.Litt., D.D.

CANON OF WESTMINSTER, FELLOW OF MERTON COLLEGE;
FELLOW OF THE BRITISH ACADEMY

WITH AN INTRODUCTION BY THE
REV. W O. E. OESTERLEY, D.D.

SOCIETY FOR PROMOTING
CHRISTIAN KNOWLEDGE
LONDON: 68, HAYMARKET, S.W.
1917

EDITORS' PREFACE

THE object of this series of translations is primarily to furnish students with short, cheap, and handy text-books, which, it is hoped, will facilitate the study of the particular texts in class under competent teachers. But it is also hoped that the volumes will be acceptable to the general reader who may be interested in the subjects with which they deal. It has been thought advisable, as a general rule, to restrict the notes and comments to a small compass, more especially as, in most cases, excellent works of a more elaborate character are available Indeed, it is much to be desired that these translations may have the effect of inducing readers to study the larger works.

Our principal aim, in a word, is to make some difficult texts, important for the study of Christian origins, more generally accessible in faithful and scholarly translations.

In most cases these texts are not available in a cheap and handy form In one or two cases texts have been included of books which are available in the official Apocrypha; but in every such case reasons exist for putting forth these texts in a new translation, with an Introduction, in this Series.

We desire to express our thanks to Canon Charles and Messrs. A. & C. Black for their permission to reprint here the translation of the *Testaments* published in 1908. With some small exceptions this is reprinted here *in extenso ;* owing to the exigencies of space we have been unable to give here the parallel columns (two, and sometimes three) representing

(c) A prophecy concerning the patriarch's posterity in the last times; in nearly each case the patriarchs foretell a falling-away of their descendants which will result in misfortune coming upon them, this takes the form, as a rule, of captivity among the Gentiles.

In some of the testaments sections of special content are introduced which have nothing at all to do with the three main topics just enumerated These sections have an interest of their own; but it may well be doubted whether they formed part of the original work. They are as follows:

The seven spirits of deceit (Reuben ii 1–iii 8).

The vision of the heavens (Levi ii 1–v. 7)

The vision of the seven men in white raiment (Levi viii. 1–18).

A Messianic hymn (Levi xviii. 2–14).

The spirits that wait upon man (Judah xx. 1–5).

The constitution of man (Naphthali ii 1–10).

The vision on the mount-of-Olives (Naphthali v. 1–8)

The vision of the wrecked-ship (Naphthali vi. 1–9).

The two ways (Asher i. 3–vi. 6)

Joseph's vision (Joseph xix. 1–12)

The good inclination (Benjamin vi. 1–7).

The sword of Beliar (Bejamin vii. 1–5).

These offer much that is of great-interest,—and should be specially studied.

The original language of the book was, in all probability, Hebrew (rather than Aramaic); but the earliest form at present known to be in existence is a Greek translation of this

HISTORICAL BACKGROUND OF THE BOOK [1]

As we shall see later on there are certain portions of the book which belong to a later date than the ground-work. In this historical survey, therefore, it will be necessary to take into consideration the

[1] For the date of our book see p. xvi

periods to which each of these parts of the book belong. It is true, the later portions do not embody many long passages of the book, but some of these are important from more than one point of view, and their significance cannot be appreciated without some clear knowledge of the history of times which they reflect.

It will be convenient to begin with the reign of Hyrcanus I, as, with the death of Judas Maccabæus in B.C. 135, the year in which Hyrcanus became ruler, what is in some sense a new epoch in Jewish history opens. Simon the Maccabee had three sons, Mattathias, Judas and John Hyrcanus; the two former were, together with their father, treacherously murdered in B.C. 135 by Ptolemy the son of Abubus,[1] *strategos* over the plain of Jericho. As the high-priesthood, together with the leadership of the nation, had been declared hereditary in the house of Simon,[2] John Hyrcanus [3] was recognized as the rightful heir. The troubles that beset Hyrcanus on becoming ruler are recorded in I Macc. xvi, and in greater detail in Josephus, *Antiq.*, XIII. vii viii., *Bell. Jud.*, I. ii. 3, 4. Ptolemy, the one just mentioned, was a less dangerous foe than the king of Syria, Antiochus VII (Sidetes), the defeat he suffered from the latter would have been more disastrous in its consequences had it not been for the friendship of the Romans, which had been acquired by the wisdom and foresight of Simon the Maccabee. But Hyrcanus' defeat by Antiochus VII showed that the independence of the small Jewish state was only conditioned by weakness in the Syrian kingdom; as soon as the Syrian king found himself free from foreign entanglements and able to undertake vigorous action in his own kingdom, he proved himself too strong, and Jewish resistance gave way. However, when

---

[1] See I Macc xvi 11-17, Josephus, *Antiq. XIII.* vii 4

[2] See I Macc xiv 41-49

[3] The name Hyrcanus is probably derived from that of the Parthian province of Hyrcania

Antiochus, in B C 128, had fallen in battle against the Parthians, Hyrcanus felt himself strong enough to assert his independence once more. For some time he was successful, but again Syria became too strong for him, and it was only owing once more to Roman friendship that he was able to hold his own in spite of defeat. So that what with the troubles of Syria on the one hand, and the friendship of Rome on the other, John Hyrcanus was enabled to rule with success over a kingdom more extensive than it had been since the days of Jeroboam II Thus Josephus is justified in regarding his reign as a prosperous one; he says that Hyrcanus "lived happily, and administered the Government in the best manner for thirty-one years . he was esteemed by God worthy of the three greatest privileges: the government of his nation, the dignity of the high-priesthood, and prophecy; for God was with him . . ."[1] On the coins of his reign the inscription runs "John the High-priest, head of the congregation (= the Church) of the Jews"; from this it is clear that the head of the Jewish State looked upon himself first and foremost as a priest, nevertheless the fact that John Hyrcanus had his name inscribed on coins (he is, as far as is known, the first high-priest of the Jews to do so) shows that he regarded himself as in some sense a king, though he did not actually assume this title, as well as high-priest. This is the first point of special importance to note.

The second point of special interest, in the present connection, that the reign of John Hyrcanus has for us is that we hear for the first time of a collision between the Pharisees and Sadducees; the passage from Josephus in which this episode is recounted is important for more than one reason; it is, therefore, worth quoting. After telling of Hyrcanus' successes which he was able to achieve on the death of Antiochus in Parthia, Josephus proceeds "How-

[1] *Antiq XIII.* x 7

ever, this prosperous state of affairs moved the Jews to envy Hyrcanus, but they that were the worst disposed to him were the Pharisees . . . . These have so great a power over the multitude, that when they say anything against the king, or against the high-priest, they are presently believed. Now Hyrcanus was a disciple of theirs, and greatly beloved by them." Then we are told of a banquet which Hyrcanus gave to the leaders of the Pharisees, when the latter spoke in high terms of their host, Hyrcanus expressed his desire to do all that was right according to the teaching of the Pharisees. Then the narrative continues: "But still there was one of his guests there, whose name was Eleazar, a man of ill temper, and delighting in seditious practices. This man said, 'Since thou desirest to know the truth, if thou wilt be righteous in earnest, lay down the high-priesthood, and content thyself with the civil government of the people.' And when he desired to know for what cause he ought to lay down the high-priesthood, the other replied, 'We have heard it from old men that thy mother had been a captive in the reign of Antiochus Epiphanes.'" This insulting, and, at the same time, untrue reflection upon Hyrcanus' descent greatly aroused his wrath; and he appealed to the Pharisees to declare what punishment was due to the man who had thus outraged the ruler's dignity. To his surprise and indignation the Pharisees replied that he deserved "bonds and stripes," Hyrcanus expecting that they would have suggested the death sentence. He, no doubt rightly, suspected that the whole thing had been got up with the purpose of ousting him from the high-priesthood, and, in consequence broke with the Pharisees entirely, going so far as "to abolish the decrees they had imposed upon the people, and to punish those that observed them."[1] Hyrcanus then definitely joined the party of the Sadducees. From this time onwards the Pharisees and Sadducees

[1] *Antiq. XIII. x. 3-6.*

appear as parties opposed politically as well as
religiously.

John Hyrcanus died in B.C. 104 and was succeeded
by his son Aristobulus I, who was the first Jewish
ruler since the days of the Monarchy to assume
definitely the title of king. After a very short reign
he died of a painful disease,[1] and his brother Alexander
Jannæus began his long reign (B.C. 102–76) He
concentrated his entire energy upon the one object
of extending the borders of his kingdom. His reign
was one long series of wars, and the duties of his
high-priesthood were wholly neglected. He died on
the battle-field. It is said that Alexander Jannæus
counselled his wife Alexandra, before he died, to
permit to the Pharisees a more extended influence ;
he doubtless realized how grossly he had neglected
his religious duties, and thus desired to make some
amends His widow Alexandra, or, according to
her Jewish name, Salome (Salma), reigned B C. 76–
67 ; the high-priestly office was conferred upon her
eldest son Hyrcanus She managed to retain the
extended boundaries of the kingdom gained by her
husband. Within the kingdom the Pharisaic party
had complete mastery.

On the death of Alexandra entirely new conditions arose, Palestine came under the suzerainty
of Rome. The Roman power would, it is true,
have asserted itself over Palestine in any case,
sooner or later, but, as a matter of fact, circum-
stances in this country, during the reign which
followed that of Alexandra, were such as to invite
the intervention of Rome. At the very end of her
reign the Sadducæan party, which had been oppressed by the dominant Pharisaic party, broke
out into revolt in Judæa. Of Alexandra's two sons
Hyrcanus upheld the Pharisaic party while Aristobulus, the younger, sided with the Sadducees. The
latter was the more vigorous of the two brothers
and gained considerable success at the outset of

[1] Josephus, *Antiq. XIII.* xi 3

this struggle. Alexandra died at the beginning of
the civil-strife. During her reign she had appointed,
as we have seen, her eldest son, Hyrcanus, to the
high-priesthood (he was, in any case, the rightful
successor), but immediately upon her death her
second son, Aristobulus, sought to gain the kingdom. He conquered his brother in battle near
Jericho, and Hyrcanus fled to Jerusalem. Hyrcanus
then made peace by renouncing both the high-
priesthood and the kingship in favour of Aristobulus. This, one would suppose, would have settled
the matter, but it was not so. Urged on by
Antipater,[1] the governor of Idumæa, Hyrcanus was
induced to fight for his rights. An alliance, brought
about by Antipater, was made between Hyrcanus
and Aretas, an Arab prince. Together they attacked
Aristobulus, and overcame him; he fled to Jerusalem,
where he was besieged.

Whilst this fratricidal struggle was going on,
Pompey had been conducting his victorious campaign in Asia. In the year B C 65 he sent one of
his generals, Scaurus, into Syria, where the latter
heard of the civil war which was taking place
in Palestine. Both brothers sent deputations to
Scaurus and sought to gain him, in the end he
decided to uphold Aristobulus. For the time being,
therefore, Aristobulus was master in Judæa. This
did not, however, last long. Pompey himself arrived
in Syria in B C 63, and while sojourning in Damascus
he was approached by three deputations of Jews;
these represented the parties of Aristobulus and
Hyrcanus respectively, and a further one representing the Jewish nation, this last wished to have
nothing to do with the two others[2] As Pompey
was about to undertake an expedition against the

---

[1] The father of Herod the Great

[2] This is important, showing, as it does, that there was at
least a considerable section of the Jews at this time which
would have nothing to do with either the Sadducæan or
Pharisaic party.

Nabatæans, he told his petitioners that they must
wait until this had been accomplished, and that
then he would decide upon what course he would
follow. On his way south, however, Pompey had
reason to suspect Aristobulus of treachery; so he
postponed his intended campaign He now commanded Aristobulus to deliver up Jerusalem; seeing
that resistance was useless Aristobulus submitted;
he left the capital and came to Pompey Thereupon Pompey sent his general, Gabinius, to take
possession of Jerusalem. Gabinius, however, returned without having accomplished his purpose,
for the defenders of Jerusalem refused to give up
the city in spite of Aristobulus' surrender. So
Pompey himself came against Jerusalem.

Now in Jerusalem itself matters were in a deplorable state, for the supporters of Aristobulus and
Hyrcanus were quarrelling amongst themselves;
those of Aristobulus determined to resist, while those
of Hyrcanus wanted to submit because they regarded Pompey as their deliverer. These latter,
being more numerous, had their way, and Pompey
was admitted into Jerusalem without having to
strike a blow. The supporters of Aristobulus, however, withdrew to the Temple mount, the position of
which was very strong; here they held out for three
months, but were ultimately compelled to surrender.

Jerusalem, together with the whole land of the
Jews, became tributary to Rome. But Judæa became greatly circumscribed; the whole coast-land
was cut off from it. as well as all the non-Jewish
cities east of the Jordan; Samaria also, together
with a large tract of country, was divided from
Judæa. What was left of Judæa was placed under
the high-priesthood of Hyrcanus II, but he was not
permitted to retain the title of king. The whole of
Syria thus became a Roman province.

From the taking of Jerusalem by Pompey in
B C. 63 to the year B C. 47, when Cæsar became
actively interested in the Jews, the lot of the people

was a hard one   But things altered in consequence
of Cæsar's gratitude to the Jews for supporting him
in his Alexandrine war   Hyrcanus II had sent
Antipater with a small Jewish army to join that of
Mithridates of Pergamum, who was on his way to
fight for Cæsar, this had the result of inducing various
other small communities in Syria to espouse Cæsar's
cause   Both Hyrcanus II and Antipater had good
reason to congratulate themselves on what they had
done, for Cæsar expressed his gratitude in the
following way   In addition to being confirmed in
the high-priesthood Hyrcanus was made temporal
ruler in Judæa with the title of Ethnarch, which was
to be hereditary, the supreme court for the admini-
stration of justice in all that related to Jewish law
was also placed under the immediate jurisdiction of
Hyrcanus, a number of cities were given back to
Judæa, including Joppa on the coast, and many
taxes were remitted   Antipater was rewarded by
being nominated Procurator of Judæa   It is, however, necessary to point out that by receiving this
office direct from Cæsar, Antipater was no more
subject to Hyrcanus, as he had been hitherto, but
was responsible to Rome alone   This is of importance for the further history of Judæa, for Antipater
was thereby enabled to increase his power   He
managed, indeed, to procure important posts for his
sons · Phasae being appointed to administer the
district of Jerusalem, and Herod that of Galilee.
On the death of Antipater both his sons were made
Tetrarchs, with the result that Hyrcanus to all
intents and purposes lost his authority as temporal
ruler   This happened in the year B C 41. In the
following year the whole condition of affairs in
Judæa became again altered owing to the invasion
of Syria by the Parthians   There is no need to go
into the details of this invasion ; the important point,
among its various consequences, is that Herod was
made king of Judæa by the Roman power. On his
death Judæa was divided up.

To sum up : by the end of the Maccabæan struggle the Jewish State enjoyed practical independence under the high-priest, the "head of the people"; for a brief while it became a kingdom. Then the whole of Syria came under Roman suzerainty, and the rulers of the different provinces received the titles of Ethnarch, Tetrarch, Procurator. Then Herod was appointed king of Judæa. On his death the whole of Syria was divided between his three sons Archelaus became Ethnarch of Judæa, Idumæa, and Samaria (cp. Matt ii 22); Antipas, who is always called Herod in the New Testament, received the title of Tetrarch (he is called "king" in Mark vi. 14), and he inherited from his father Galilee and Peræa; Philip was made Tetrarch of Northern Palestine.

DATE OF THE BOOK

The date of the book in its original form is not difficult to define within fairly close limits, as the following quotations will show:

Test. Reuben vi. 10–12 . "And draw ye near to Levi in humbleness of heart, that ye may receive a blessing from his mouth. For he shall bless Israel and Judah, because him hath the Lord chosen to be king over all the nation. And bow down before his seed, for on our behalf it will die in wars visible and invisible, and will be among you an eternal king."

Test. Simeon v. 5 : "But they shall not be able to withstand Levi; for he shall wage the war of the Lord, and shall conquer all your hosts."

In speaking of Levi the writer refers, of course, to the high-priest; and the high-priest is spoken of as having been chosen king by the Lord; he is also spoken of as one who "shall wage the war of the Lord." This combination of high-priest, king, and warrior can only be in reference to the Maccabæan priest-kings. But, further, in *Test. Levi* viii. 11–15, it is said : "Levi, thy seed shall be divided into three offices, for a sign of the glory of the Lord who

is to come   And the first portion shall be great,
yea, greater than it shall none be   The second shall
be in the priesthood   And the third shall be called
by a new name, because a king shall arise in Judah,
and shall establish a new priesthood, after the fashion
of the Gentiles   And his presence is beloved, as a
prophet of the Most High, of the seed of Abraham
our father." Here we have the reference to king,
priest and prophet, all centred in one person, taking
this with the quotation from Josephus given above
(p x), who speaks of John Hyrcanus as possessor
of the three greatest privileges, " the government of
his nation, the dignity of the high-priesthood, and
prophecy," it is clear that this is the ruler referred
to in this passage, because no other in all Jewish
history combined these three offices in himself   In
regard to the " new name," spoken of in the passage
quoted, Charles points out that the Maccabæan
high-priests " were the first Jewish priests to assume
the title ' priests of the Most High God ' This title,
anciently borne by Melchizedek (Gen xiv. 18), was
revived by the new holders of the high-priesthood
when they displaced the Zadokite priesthood, the
legitimate holders of the office   The title is found
in the Book of Jubilees, the Assumption of Moses,
the Talmud and Josephus [1] A kindred title of the
same significance appears in Ps cx, where the priest-
king, taken by a growing number of expositors to be
Simon the Maccabee, is addressed as a priest for
ever after the order of Melchizedek   In due accord
with this, our text declares that a new name should
mark the new priesthood " [2] In Test Levi viii. 14,
15, then, this is applied to John Hyrcanus, he
reigned, as we have seen, B C 135-104, our book
in its original form may, therefore, well belong to
this period, but the possibility of a rather later

---

[1] Book of Jub. xxxii 1, xxxii 16, Assumption of Moses
vi 1, Josephus, *Antiq. XVI.* vi 2, and in the Talmud, Rosh
ha-shanah 18b

[2] *The Testaments of the Twelve Patriarchs*, pp li f (1908).

B

date is not excluded. Some later portions of the book were added during the middle of the last century B.C., with the purpose of denouncing what had become the degenerate Maccabæan high-priesthood. We saw in the preceding section that during the reign of Alexander Jannæus the duties of the high-priesthood were wholly neglected, and that on the death of Alexandra the general conditions of the land, both spiritual and civil, were deplorable. It was owing to this that the later additions were made; Charles, with every justification, regards the following passages as comprising these: Test Levi x, xiv.–xvi, Test. Judah xvii 2–xviii. 1 (?), xxi. 6–xxiii, xxiv 4–6, Test. Zebulun ix ; Test. Dan v. 6, 7, vii. 3 (?); Test. Naphtali iv.; Test. Gad viii. 2; Test. Asher vii. 4–7. In the case of Test Levi xiv. 4, he says that it "refers undeniably to Alexander Jannæus, for this very fact is recounted of him by Josephus"[1] (*Antiq.* XIII, xiv. 2). A few other passages are probably also of later date[2] Another set of passages of later date have a special interest of their own, viz. the Christian additions; these are, almost always, easily discerned, their Christian character being obvious, *e. g* Test Simeon vi. 7, vii 2; Test. Levi xiv. 2; Test. Dan vi 9; Test. Asher vii. 3; Test. Benjamin iii. 8, ix. 3–5. A full list of these is given by Charles, *op cit.*, pp. 61–65.

AUTHORSHIP

The question of Authorship is difficult. At the time when the ground-work of the book was written it is questionable whether the distinctive doctrinal differences between the Pharisees and Sadducees had already become sufficiently marked to enable us to say with certitude whether the standpoint in the book is either Pharisaic or Sadducæan. The Law and the Temple services are strongly upheld,

[1] *Op cit*, p. 58.   [2] See Charles, *op. cit*, pp 59 ff.

and the Messianic kingdom is believed in, this
might have been equally the standpoint of a Pharisee
or a Sadducee, though it must be said that the
specifically Pharisaic attitude as to the Law is not
to be found in the book Moreover, nothing could
be more un-Pharisaic than the spirit so often mani-
fested, and well described by Charles (though he
believes the ground-work to have been the work of
a Pharisee of the *Chasid* type) in the words: " A
true son of the larger-hearted Old Testament prophets
he proclaims the salvation of the Gentiles The
promised time has come The kingdom is already
established, and all the Gentiles will be saved through
Israel In the Judgement the conduct of the best
heathen will form the norm according to which Israel
will be judged " [1] Such an universalistic spirit is
wholly alien to the Pharisaic outlook upon the world.
A strong case has been made out for Sadducæan
authorship,[2] and when one thinks of the deeply
religious elements in the *Wisdom of Ben-Sira*, which
admittedly emanated from " Sadducæan " circles
(*i e.* circles from which, in later times, the Sadducees
as a party developed), and notices the many points
of similarity in the general religious attitude between
it and the *Testaments*, one sees the justice and strength
of this contention. What undoubtedly gives a
Pharisaic tone to the book is the fact that it has
been worked over by a later Pharisaic editor, but
the ground-work of the book does not show any
specifically Pharisaic *traits*. The exhortations to
peace and brotherly kindness which so often occur
in the book show that the author yearned for a
spirit of brotherly kindness, which presumably did
not exist ; hence it is possible that the party wrangles
between Sadducees and Pharisees may have prompted
a peace-loving Sadducee to appeal in this way for a
better understanding between the two parties But
after all, it is just possible that the book was origin-
ally written by a good Jew, neither Sadducæan nor

[1] Leszynsky, *Die Sadduzäer*, pp 239 ff   [2] *Op cit.*, p xcvii

Pharisaic, who loved all that was best among his people.

Charles believes, though with some hesitation, in unity of authorship so far as the ground-work of the book is concerned, though it presents, "it must be confessed, a want of coherence at times, and the parts dealing with the duty of submission to Levi, or to Levi and Judah jointly, come in occasionally very abruptly." That is certainly so, and it is also true of some other passages; nevertheless, in reading the book carefully through most people will be inclined to agree with Charles; though it is possible that the ground-work does not comprise as much as eleven-twelfths of the *Testaments*, after the removal of the Jewish and Christian additions, as Charles holds.

Importance of the Book for the Study of Christian Origins

There are some sayings of Christ which should be borne in mind when reading a pre-Christian work such as this; for in face of the teaching of certain passages in this book, which clearly belong to it in its original form—the whole context shows them to be integral parts of the book—some people may be inclined to ask where the originality of Christ's ethical teaching comes in if before Him there existed Jewish teachers whose ethical teaching appears to be on a level with that of the Gospel. The sayings of our Lord referred to are the following—and there are others of similar import:

"Think not that I came to destroy the law or the prophets; I came not to destroy, but to fulfil" (Matt. v. 17).

"Therefore every scribe who hath been made a disciple to the kingdom of heaven is like unto a man that is a householder, which bringeth forth out of his treasure things new and old" (Matt. xiii. 52).

"The scribes and the Pharisees sit on Moses' seat;

all things therefore whatsoever they bid you, these
do and observe ." (Matt xxiii 1–3)

Whatever else passages of this kind may teach,
there can be no doubt that they show that Christ
fully recognized both the permanent good in what
earlier teachers had taught, as well as the authorita-
tive character of much that had been taught. The
originality of Christ's teaching, which is abundantly
clear from the Gospel records, did not prevent Him
from incorporating into His teaching much that was
good in what earlier teachers had taught. To speak
of the influence of earlier writings upon Christ is
incorrect because there could be no scope for such
influence to be exercised upon One in Whom was all
knowledge and understanding, but that does not
mean to say that Christ would not have utilized the
writings and teachings of others, especially if (as
was very probably the case) a knowledge of the
contents of such writings was current among the
people This should be borne in mind in reading
the following extracts, chosen from a number of
similar import, which reveal an astonishingly high
ethical standard in the pre-Christian parts of our
book

" Love the Lord with all your life, and one another
with a true heart " (Test. Dan v. 3; cp Matt xxii.
37–39)

"Love ye one another from the heart, and if a
man sin against thee, speak peaceably to him, and
in thy soul hold not guile, and if he repent and
confess, forgive him ... But if he be shameless
and persisteth in his wrong-doing even so forgive
him from the heart, and leave to God the avenging "
(Test Gad vi 3, 7; see also vii 7; cp Matt xviii.
35, Luke xvii 3). Similar teaching is contained in
another long and striking passage (Test. Gad iv, v.),
one or two verses from which are worth quoting.
"For the spirit of hatred worketh together with Satan,
through hastiness of spirit, in all things unto men's
death, but the spirit of love worketh together with

the law of God in long-suffering unto the salvation
of men. . . . Righteousness casteth out hatred,
humility destroyeth envy For he that is just and
humble is ashamed to do what is unjust, being reproved not of another, but of his own heart, because
the Lord looketh upon his inclination He speaketh
not against a holy man, because the fear of God
overcometh hatred. For fearing lest he should
offend the Lord, he will not do wrong to any man,
even in thought."

Ethical teaching of this kind is as exalted as much
that we read in the Gospels; and there is every reason
for believing that such teaching was not restricted to
favoured circles, but that it was given, as opportunity offered, to the people at large That similar
teaching is found in the Gospels shows that Christ
was ready to receive and so hand on whatever was
truly good in that which earlier teachers had
taught

There are many other passages in this book which
show such close affinity in thought and language
with what we read in the Gospels that it is difficult
not to believe that Christ was familiar with our
book, and willingly made use of it sometimes in His
teaching. Of the large number of such passages,[1]
the following one offers a good example

" I was sold into slavery, and the Lord of all made
          me free ;
      I was taken into captivity, and His strong hand
          succoured me.
      I was beset with hunger, and the Lord Himself
          nourished me ,
      I was alone, and God comforted me ;
      I was sick, and the Lord visited me ;
      I was in prison, and my God showed favour
          unto me ;
      In bonds, and He released me   " (Test.
          Joseph 1 5–6; cp Matt xxv. 35, 36, and in

---

[1] A very useful list is given by Charles, op cit , pp lxxviii, ff

connection with these two passages one should recall Matt. v. 48 . " Ye, therefore, shall be perfect, as your heavenly Father is perfect "). For the doctrinal teaching of the book see Charles, *op. cit* , pp. xcii –xcix., and for the bibliography pp. 28–41, and *Schürer, Geschichte des Jüdischen Volkes*, iii. pp. 352–356 (1909).

THE TESTAMENTS OF
THE TWELVE PATRIARCHS

THE TESTAMENT OF REUBEN, THE FIRST-BORN SON OF JACOB AND LEAH

I 1-10.   Introduction   Reuben's Confession and Repentance

1. THE copy of the Testament of Reuben, even the commands which he gave his sons ⌐before he died in the hundred and twenty-fifth year of his life ⌐ 2. Two years after the death of Joseph ⌐his brother⌐, when Reuben fell ill, his sons and his sons' sons were gathered together to visit him   3. And he said to them : My children, behold I am dying, and go the way of my fathers   4. And seeing ⌐there⌐ Judah, and Gad and Asher, his brethren, he said to them Raise me up, that I may tell to my brethren and to my children what things I have hidden in my heart, for behold now at length I am passing away.   5. And he arose and kissed them, and said unto them : Hear, my brethren, and do ye, my children, give ear to Reuben your father, in the commands which I give you   6. And behold I call to witness against you this day the God of heaven, that ye walk not in the ignorance of youth and fornication, wherein I was poured out, and defiled the bed of my father Jacob   7. And I tell you that He smote me with a sore plague in my loins for seven months , and had not my father Jacob prayed for me to the Lord, the

Lord would have destroyed me. 8. For I was thirty years old when I wrought the evil thing before the Lord, and for seven months I was sick unto death. 9. And after this I repented with set purpose of my soul for seven years before the Lord 10. And wine and strong drink I drank not, and flesh entered not into my mouth, and I ate no pleasant food; but I mourned over my sin, for it was great, such as had not been in Israel.

II. 1–III. 8. The Seven Spirits of Deceit

II. And now hear me, my children, what things I saw concerning the seven spirits of deceit, when I repented. 2. Seven spirits therefore are appointed against man, and they are the leaders in the works of youth.

3 [And seven other spirits are given to him at his creation, that through them should be done every work of man. 4. The first is the spirit of life, with which the constitution (of man) is created. The second is the sense of sight, with which ariseth desire. 5. The third is the sense of hearing, with which cometh teaching. The fourth is the sense of smell, with which tastes are given to draw air and breath. 6. The fifth is the power of speech, with which cometh knowledge. 7. The sixth is the sense of taste, with which cometh the eating of meats and drinks; and by it strength is produced, for in food is the foundation of strength. 8. The seventh is the power of procreation and sexual intercourse, with which through love of pleasure sins enter in. 9 Wherefore it is the last in order of creation, and the first in that of youth, because it is filled with ignorance, and leadeth the youth as a blind man to a pit, and as a beast to a precipice.

III. Besides all these there is an eighth spirit of sleep, with which is brought about the trance of nature and the image of death. 2. With these spirits are mingled the spirits of error.]

3 First, the spirit of fornication is seated in the

nature and in the senses, the second, the spirit of
insatiableness, in the belly, 4 The third, the spirit
of fighting, in the liver and gall. The fourth is the
spirit of obsequiousness and chicanery, that through
officious attention one may be fair in seeming.
5. The fifth is the spirit of pride, that one may be
boastful and arrogant. The sixth is the spirit of
lying, in perdition and in jealousy to practise deceits,
and concealments from kindred and friends. 6 The
seventh is the spirit of injustice, with which are
thefts and acts of rapacity, that a man may fulfil
the desire of his heart; for injustice worketh together
with the other spirits by the taking of gifts. [7 And
with all these the spirit of sleep is joined which is
(that) of error and fantasy] 8 And so perisheth every
young man, darkening his mind from the truth, and not
understanding the law of God, nor obeying the admoni-
tions of his fathers, as befell me also in my youth

III 9–15 Reuben's Sin

9 And now, my children, love the truth, and it
will preserve you hear ye ⌜the words of⌝ Reuben
your father.
10. Pay no heed to the face of a woman,
    Nor associate with another man's wife,
    Nor meddle with affairs of womankind.
11 For had I not seen Bilhah bathing in a covered
place, I had not fallen into this great iniquity. 12 For
my mind taking in the thought of the woman's
nakedness, suffered me not ⌜to sleep⌝ until I had
wrought the abominable thing 13 For while Jacob
our father had gone to Isaac his father, when we were
in Eder, near to Ephrath in Bethlehem, Bilhah became drunk and was asleep uncovered in her chamber
14 Having therefore gone in and beheld her nakedness, I wrought the impiety ⌜without her perceiving
it⌝, and leaving her sleeping I departed. 15 And
forthwith an angel of God revealed to my father concerning my impiety, and he came and mourned over
me, and touched her no more

IV. 1–VI. 4. A Warning against Sin

IV. Pay no heed, therefore, ⌜my children⌝, to the beauty of women, nor set your mind on their affairs; but walk in singleness of heart in the fear of the Lord, and expend labour on good works, and on study and on your flocks, until the Lord give you a wife, whom He will, that ye suffer not as I did. 2. For until my father's death I had not boldness to look in his face, or to speak to any of my brethren, because of the reproach. 3. Even until now my conscience causeth me anguish on account of my impiety 4. And yet my father comforted me much, and prayed for me unto the Lord, that the anger of the Lord might pass from me, even as the Lord showed And thenceforth until now I have been on my guard and sinned not. 5. Therefore, my children, ⌜I say unto you⌝, observe ⌜all⌝ things whatsoever I command you, and ye shall not sin 6 For a pit unto the soul is the sin of fornication, separating it from God, and bringing it near to idols, because it deceiveth the mind and understanding, and leadeth down young men into Hades before their time 7 For many hath fornication destroyed; because, though a man be old or noble, ⌜or rich or poor⌝, he bringeth reproach upon himself with the sons of men and derision with Beliar 8 For hear ye regarding Joseph how he guarded himself from a woman, and purged his thoughts from all fornication, and found favour in the sight of God and men. 9 For the Egyptian woman did many things unto him, and summoned magicians, and offered him love potions, but the purpose of his soul admitted no evil desire 10. Therefore the God of your fathers delivered him from every evil (and) hidden death. 11. For if fornication overcomes not your mind, neither can Beliar overcome you

V ⌜For⌝ evil are women, my children; and since they have no power or strength over man, they use wiles by outward attractions that they may draw him to themselves. 2. And whom they cannot

bewitch by outward attractions, him they overcome
by craft   3 ⌐For⌐ moreover, concerning them, the
angel of the Lord told me, and taught me, that
women are overcome by the spirit of fornication
more than men, and in their heart they plot against
men , and by means of their adornment they deceive
first their minds, and by the glance of the eye instil
the poison, and then through the accomplished act
they take them captive   4 For a woman cannot force
a man openly, but by a harlot's bearing she beguiles
him   5 Flee, therefore, fornication, my children,
and command your wives and your daughters, that
they adorn not their heads and faces to deceive the
mind , because every woman who useth these wiles
hath been reserved for eternal punishment   6 For
thus they allured the Watchers who were before the
flood, for as these continually beheld them, they
lusted after them, and they conceived the act in their
mind ; for they changed themselves into the shape of
men, and appeared to them when they were with
their husbands   7. And the women lusting in their
minds after their forms, gave birth to giants, for the
Watchers appeared to them as reaching even unto
heaven

VI Beware, therefore, of fornication ; and if you
wish to be pure in mind, guard your senses from every
woman.   2 And command the women likewise not
to associate with men, that they also may be pure in
mind   3 For constant meetings, even though the
ungodly deed be not wrought, are to them an irre-
mediable disease, and to us a destruction of Beliar
and an eternal reproach   4 For in fornication there
is neither understanding nor godliness, and all
jealousy dwelleth in the lust thereof.

VI. 5–12 An Exhortation to obey Levi, in whom is vested a Royal Priesthood

5. Therefore, ⌐then, I say unto you,⌐ ye will be
jealous ⌐against the sons of Levi⌐, and will seek to be
exalted over them ; but ye shall not be able.   6. For

God will avenge them ⌐and ye shall die by an evil death⌐. 7 For to Levi God gave the sovereignty [and to Judah with him and to me also, and to Dan and Joseph, that we should be for rulers] 8. Therefore I command you to hearken to Levi, because he shall know the law of the Lord, and shall give ordinances for judgement and shall sacrifice for all Israel until the consummation of the times, as the anointed High Priest, of whom the Lord spake 9 I adjure you by the God of heaven to do truth each one unto his neighbour and to entertain love each for his brother 10 And draw ye near to Levi in humbleness of heart, that ye may receive a blessing from his mouth 11. For he shall bless Israel and Judah, because him hath the Lord chosen to be king over all the nation 12 And bow down before his seed, for on our behalf it will die in wars visible and invisible, and will be among you an eternal king

VII 1-2. Reuben's Death and Burial

VII. And Reuben died, having given these commands to his sons. 2 And they placed him in a coffin until they carried him up from Egypt, and buried him ⌐in Hebron⌐ in the cave where his father was.

THE TESTAMENT OF SIMEON, THE SECOND SON OF JACOB AND LEAH

I 1-II 14. Introduction. Simeon's Confession and Repentance

I. THE copy of the words of Simeon, the things which he spake to his sons before he died, in the hundred and twentieth year of his life, at which time Joseph, ⌐his brother,⌐ died 2. For when Simeon was sick, his sons came to visit him, and he strengthened himself and sat up and kissed them, and said

11 Hearken, my children, to Simeon your father,
And I will declare unto you what things I have in my heart.

2 I was born of Jacob as my father's second son,
And my mother Leah called me Simeon,
Because the Lord had heard her prayer

3 Moreover, I became strong exceedingly,
I shrank from no achievement,
Nor was I afraid of ought

4 For my heart was hard,
And my liver was immovable,
And my bowel without compassion

5. Because valour also hath been given from the Most High to men in soul and body 6. For in the time of my youth I was jealous ⌐in many things⌐ of Joseph, because my father loved him ⌐beyond all⌐ 7 And I set my mind against him to destroy him, because the prince of deceit sent forth the spirit of jealousy and blinded my mind, so that I regarded him not as a brother, nor did I spare even Jacob my father. 8 But his God and the God of his fathers sent forth His angel, and delivered him out of my hands 9. For when I went to Shechem to bring ointment for the flocks, and Reuben to Dothan, where were our necessaries and all our stores, Judah my brother sold him to the Ishmaelites 10. And when Reuben heard these things he was grieved, for he wished to restore him to his father 11 But on hearing this I was ⌐exceedingly⌐ wroth against Judah in that he let him go away alive, and for five months I continued wrathful against him 12 But the Lord restrained me, and withheld ⌐from me⌐ the power of my hands; for my right hand was half withered for seven days 13 And I knew, my children, that because of Joseph this had befallen me, and I repented and wept, and I besought the Lord God that my hand might be restored, and that I might hold aloof from all pollution

and envy, ⌐and from all folly¬. 14. For I knew that
I had devised an evil thing before the Lord and Jacob
my father, on account of Joseph my brother, in that
I envied him.

III 1–6. The Evil of Envy, and its Cure

III. And now, my children, ⌐hearken unto me and¬
beware of the spirit of deceit and of envy. 2. For
envy ruleth over the whole mind of a man, and suf-
fereth him ⌐neither to eat nor to drink¬, nor to do
any good thing. 3. But it ever suggesteth (to him)
to destroy him that he envieth, and so long as he
that is envied flourisheth, he that envieth fadeth
away. 4. Two years ⌐therefore¬ I afflicted my soul
with fasting in the fear of the Lord, and I learnt that
deliverance from envy cometh by the fear of God.
5. For if a man flee to the Lord, the evil spirit runneth
away from him, and his mind is lightened. 6. And
henceforward he sympathiseth with him whom he
envied and agreeth with those who love him, and so
ceaseth from his envy.

IV. 1–7. Joseph's Good Example

IV. And my father asked ⌐concerning me¬, because he saw that I was sad, and I said unto him,
I am pained in my liver. 2. For I mourned more
than they all, because I was guilty of the selling of
Joseph. 3. And when we went down into Egypt,
and he bound me as a spy, I knew that I was suffering
justly, and I grieved not. 4 Now Joseph was a good
man, and had the Spirit of God within him : being
compassionate and pitiful, he bore no malice against
me ; but loved me even as the rest of his brethren.
5. Beware, therefore, my children, of all jealousy
and envy, and walk in singleness of heart, that God
may give ⌐you also¬ grace and glory, and blessing
upon your heads, even as ye saw in Joseph's case.
6. All his days he reproached us not concerning this
thing, but loved us as his own soul, and beyond his
own sons glorified us, and gave us riches, and cattle

and fruits   7 Do ye also, my children, love each
one his brother with a good heart, and the spirit of
envy will withdraw from you.

IV 8-9   The Evil of Envy

8. For this maketh savage the soul and destroyeth
the body; it causes anger and war in the mind, and
stirreth up unto deeds of blood, and leadeth the mind
into frenzy, [and causeth tumult to the soul and
trembling to the body]   9. For even in sleep some
malicious jealousy, deluding him, gnaweth, and with
wicked spirits disturbeth his soul, and causeth the
body to be troubled, and waketh the mind from
sleep in confusion, and as a wicked and poisonous
spirit, so appeareth it to men

V. 1.   The Comeliness of Joseph

V. Therefore was Joseph comely in appearance, and
goodly to look upon, because no wickedness dwelt in
him; for some of the trouble of the spirit the face
manifesteth.

V. 2-3.   An Exhortation to Goodness

2. And now, my children,
   Make your hearts good before the Lord,
   And your ways straight before men,
   And ye shall find grace before the Lord and
      men.
3. Beware, therefore, of fornication,
   For fornication is mother of all evils,
   Separating from God, and bringing near to
      Beliar.

V. 4-6.   Levi is to wage the War of the Lord

4. I have seen it inscribed in the writing of Enoch
that your sons shall be corrupted in fornication, and
shall do harm to the sons of Levi with the sword.
5 But they shall not be able to withstand Levi; for
he shall wage the war of the Lord, and shall conquer
⌜all⌝ your hosts.   6. And they shall be few in number,

C

divided in Levi and Judah, and there shall be none of you for sovereignty, even as also our father prophesied in his blessings.

VI 1-7. The Blessedness of Simeon's Posterity if Sin be avoided

VI Behold I have told you all things, that I may be acquitted of your sin 2 Now, if ye remove from you your envy and all stiff-neckedness,

As a rose shall my bones flourish in Israel,
And as a lily my flesh in Jacob,
And my odour shall be as the odour of Libanus;
And as cedars shall holy ones be multiplied from me for ever,
And their branches shall stretch afar off

3 Then shall perish the seed of Canaan,
And a remnant shall not be unto Amalek,
ᒥAnd all the Cappadocians shall perish,ᒧ
And all the Hittites shall be utterly destroyed

4 Then shall fail the land of Ham,
And all the people shall perish.
Then shall all the earth rest from trouble,
And all the world under heaven from war.

5. Then shall a sign be glorified greatly unto Israel,
For the Lord God appearing on earth shall come [as man],
And saving through him man.

6 Then shall all the spirits of deceit be given to be trodden under foot,
And men shall rule over wicked spirits.

7. Then shall I arise in joy,
And will bless the Most High because of His marvellous works,
[Because God hath taken a body and eaten with men and saved men].

VII. 1-3 An Exhortation to obey Levi and Judah

VII. And now, my children, obey Levi and Judah, and be not lifted up against these two tribes, for

from them shall arise unto you the salvation ˹of God˺
2 For the Lord shall raise up from Levi as it were a₁
High-priest, and from Judah as it were a King ˹God
and man], He shall save all ˹the Gentiles and] the race₁
of Israel   3. Therefore I give you these commands
that ye also may command your children, that they
may observe them throughout their generations

VIII 1-IX 2   Death and Burial of Simeon

VIII And when Simeon had made an end of commanding his sons, he slept with his fathers, being an
hundred and twenty years old   2 And they laid
him in a wooden coffin, to take up his bones to Hebron
And they took them up secretly during a war of the
Egyptians   3 For the bones of Joseph the Egyptians₁
guarded in the tombs of the Kings   4 For the
sorcerers told them, that on the departure of the
bones of Joseph there should be throughout all the
land darkness and gloom, and an exceeding great
plague to the Egyptians, so that even with a lamp a
man should not recognise his brother.

IX And the sons of Simeon bewailed their father
2 And they were in Egypt until the day of their
departure by the hand of Moses.

THE TESTAMENT OF LEVI, THE THIRD SON
OF JACOB AND LEAH

I 1-2   Introduction

I THE copy of the words of Levi, the things which
he ordained unto his sons, according to all that they
should do, and what things should befall them until
the day of judgement   2 He was sound in health
when he called them to him , for it had been revealed
to him that he should die And when they were
gathered together he said to them

II. 1–V. 7. The Vision of the Heavens

II. I, Levi, was born in Haran, and I came with my father to Shechem. 2 And I was young, about twenty years of age, when, with Simeon, I wrought vengeance on Hamor for our sister Dinah. 3 And when I was feeding the flocks in Abel-Maul, the spirit of understanding of the Lord came upon me, and I saw all men corrupting their way, and that unrighteousness had built for itself walls, and lawlessness sat upon towers. 4 And I was grieving for the race of the sons of men, and I prayed to the Lord that I might be saved. 5. Then there fell upon me a sleep, and I beheld a high mountain, and I was upon it. 6. And behold the heavens were opened, and an angel of God said to me, Levi, enter 7 And I entered from the first heaven, and I saw there a great sea hanging 8 And further, I saw a second heaven far brighter and more brilliant, for there was a boundless height also therein. 9 And I said to the angel, Why is this so ?   And the angel said to me, Marvel not at this, for thou shalt see another heaven more brilliant and incomparable

10. And when thou hast ascended thither,
      Thou shalt stand near the Lord,
      And shalt be His minister,
      And shalt declare His mysteries to men,
      And shalt proclaim concerning Him that shall
         redeem Israel

11 And by thee and Judah shall the Lord appear
         among men,
      ⌐Saving every race of men⌐.

12 And from the Lord's portion shall be thy life,
      And He shall be thy field and vineyard,
      And fruits, gold, and silver.

III. Hear, therefore, regarding the heavens which have been shown to thee The lowest is for this cause gloomy unto thee, in that it beholds all the unrighteous deeds of men. 2. And it has fire, snow, and ice made ready for the day of judgement,

in the righteous judgement of God, for in it are all
the spirits of the retributions for vengeance on men.
3. And in the second are the hosts of the armies
which are ordained for the day of judgement, to work
vengeance on the spirits of deceit and of Beliar   And
above them are the holy ones.   4. And in the highest
of all dwelleth the Great Glory, far above all holiness.
5. In [the heaven next to] it are the archangels, who
minister and make propitiation to the Lord for all the
sins of ignorance of the righteous, 6. Offering to the
Lord a sweet-smelling savour, a reasonable and a
bloodless offering   7. And [in the heaven below this]
are the angels who bear answers to the angels of the
presence of the Lord   8. And in the heaven next to
this are thrones and dominions, in which always they
offer praise to God   9. When, therefore, the Lord
looketh upon us, all of us are shaken, yea, the heavens,
and the earth, and the abysses are shaken at the
presence of His majesty   10. But the sons of men,
having no perception of these things, sin and provoke
the Most High

IV. Now, therefore, know that the Lord shall
execute judgement upon the sons of men.

> Because when the rocks are being rent,
> And the sun quenched,
> And the waters dried up,
> And the fire cowering,
> And all creation troubled,
> And the invisible spirits melting away,
> And Hades taketh spoils through the visitations
>   of the Most High,
> Men will be unbelieving and persist in their
>   iniquity.
> On this account with punishment shall they be
>   judged.

2. ᴵTherefore¹ the Most High hath heard thy
>   prayer,
> To separate thee from iniquity, and that thou
>   shouldest become to Him a son,
> And a servant, and a minister of His presence

3. The light of knowledge shalt thou light up in
   Jacob,
   And as the sun shalt thou be to all the seed of
   Israel.
4. And there shall be given to thee a blessing, and
   to all thy seed,
   Until the Lord shall visit all the Gentiles in His
   tender mercies for ever.
5 ⌜And⌝ therefore there have been given to thee
   counsel and understanding,
   That thou mightest instruct thy sons concerning
   this ;
6 Because they that bless Him shall be blessed,
   And they that curse Him shall perish.

V. And thereupon the angel opened to me the gates
of heaven, and I saw the holy temple, and upon a
throne of glory the Most High. 2. And He said to
me : Levi, I have given thee the blessings of the
priesthood until I come and sojourn in the midst
of Israel. 3 Then the angel brought me down to
the earth, and gave me a shield and a sword, and said
to me : Execute vengeance on Shechem because of
Dinah, thy sister, and I will be with thee because
the Lord hath sent me. 4. And I destroyed at that
time the sons of Hamor, as it is written in the heavenly
tablets. 5. And I said to him : I pray Thee, O lord,
tell me Thy name, that I may call upon Thee in a day
of tribulation. 6 And he said : I am the angel who
intercedeth for the nation of Israel that they may not
be smitten utterly, for every evil spirit attacketh
it. 7. And after these things I awaked, and blessed
the Most High, and the angel who intercedeth for the
nation of Israel and for all the righteous.

VI 1–VII 3 Retribution upon Shechem

VI. And when I was going to my father, I found a
brazen shield ; wherefore also the name of the mountain is Aspis, which is near Gebal, to the south of
Abila. 2. And I kept these words in my heart. And

after this I counselled my father, and Reuben my
brother, to bid the sons of Hamor not to be circum-
cised, for I was jealous because of the abomination
which they had wrought on my sister 4 And I
slew Shechem first, and Simeon slew Hamor 5 And
after this my brothers came and smote ⌈that⌉ city
with the edge of the sword 6 And my father heard
⌈these things⌉ and was wroth; and he was grieved
in that they had received the circumcision, and after
that had been put to death, and in his blessings he
looked amiss upon us 7 For we sinned because
we had done this thing against his will, and he was
sick on that day 8 But I saw that the sentence
of God was for evil upon Shechem, for they sought
to do to Sarah ⌈and Rebecca⌉ as they had done to
Dinah our sister, but the Lord prevented them 9
And they persecuted Abraham our father when he was
a stranger, and they vexed his flocks when they were
big with young, and Eblaen, who was born in his
house, they most shamefully handled 10 And thus
they did to all strangers, taking away their wives
by force, and they banished them. 11 But the wrath
of the Lord came upon them to the uttermost.

VII And I said to my father Jacob : By thee will
the Lord destroy the Canaanites, and will give their
land to thee and to thy seed after thee. 2 For from
this day forward shall Shechem be called a city of
imbeciles ; for as a man mocketh a fool, so did we
mock them, 3 Because also they had wrought folly
in Israel by defiling my sister And we departed
and came to Bethel

VIII. 1-18   The Vision of the Seven Men
in White Raiment

VIII And there again I saw a vision even as the
former, after we had spent there seventy days. 2.
And I saw seven men in white raiment saying unto
me Arise, put on the robe of the priesthood, and the
crown of righteousness, and the breastplate of under-

standing, and the garment of truth, and the plate of
faith, and the turban of the head, and the ephod
of prophecy. 3. And they severally carried (these
things) and put (them) on me, and said unto me :
From henceforth become a priest of the Lord, thou
and thy seed for ever. 4 And the first anointed me
with holy oil, and gave to me the staff of judgement.
5. The second washed me with pure water, and fed
me with bread and wine (even) the most holy things,
and clad me with a holy and glorious robe. 6 The
third clothed me with a linen vestment like an ephod.
7. The fourth put round me a girdle like unto purple.
8 The fifth gave me a branch of rich olive. 9. The
sixth placed a crown on my head. 10. The seventh
placed on my head a diadem of priesthood, and filled
my hands with incense, that I might serve as priest
to the Lord God. 11. And they said to me . Levi,
thy seed shall be divided into three offices, for a sign
of the glory of the Lord who is to come 12. And
the first portion shall be great ; yea, greater than it
shall none be 13. The second shall be in the priesthood. 14. And the third shall be called by a new
name, because a king shall arise in Judah, and shall
establish a new priesthood, after the fashion of the
Gentiles [to all the Gentiles]. 15. And his presence is
beloved, as a prophet of the Most High, of the seed of
Abraham our father.

16. Therefore, every desirable thing in Israel shall
     be for thee and for thy seed,
   And ye shall eat everything fair to look upon,
   And the table of the Lord shall thy seed appor-
     tion

17. And some of them shall be high priests, and
     judges, and scribes ;
   For by their mouth shall the holy place be
     guarded.

18. And when I awoke, I understood that this
(dream) was like the first dream. 19. And I hid
this also in my heart, and told it not to any man
upon the earth.

IX 1-14   Isaac's Instruction to Levi

IX. And after two days I and Judah went up with
our father Jacob to Isaac our father's father. 2. And
my father's father blessed me according to all the
words of the visions which I had seen. And he would
not come with us to Bethel. 3. ⌐And when we came
to Bethel⌐, my father Jacob saw a vision concerning
me, that I should be their priest unto God 4 And
he rose up early in the morning, and paid tithes of
all ⌐to the Lord⌐ through me 5 And ⌐so⌐ we came
to Hebron to dwell there. 6. And Isaac called me
continually to put me in remembrance of the law of
the Lord, even as the angel of the Lord showed unto
me   7 And he taught me the law of the priesthood,
of sacrifices, whole burnt-offerings, first-fruits, free-
will-offerings, peace-offerings   8 And each day he
was instructing me, and was busied on my behalf
before the Lord, and said to me · 9 Beware of the
spirit of fornication; for this shall continue and shall
by thy seed pollute the holy place   10. Take, therefore, to thyself a wife without blemish or pollution,
while yet thou art young, and not of the race of
strange nations   11 And before entering into the
holy place, bathe, and when thou offerest the
sacrifice, wash; and again, when thou finishest the
sacrifice, wash   12. Of twelve trees having leaves
offer to the Lord, as Abraham taught me also.   13
And of every clean beast ⌐and bird⌐ offer a sacrifice
to the Lord.   14 And of all thy first-fruits and of
wine offer the first, as a sacrifice to the Lord God;
and every sacrifice thou shalt salt with salt

X. 1-5.   Levi's Prophecy concerning his Posterity

X. Now, therefore, observe whatsoever I command
you, children, for whatsoever things I have heard
from my fathers ⌐I have declared unto you.   2. And
behold,⌐ I am clear from your ungodliness and trans-
gression, which ye shall commit in the end of the ages

[against the Saviour of the world, Christ, acting godlessly], deceiving Israel, and stirring up against it great evils from the Lord. 3. And ye shall deal lawlessly together with Israel, so He shall not bear with Jerusalem because of your wickedness; but the veil of the temple shall be rent, so as not to cover your shame 4. And ye shall be scattered as captives among the Gentiles, and shall be for a reproach and for a curse there. 5 For the house which the Lord shall choose shall be called Jerusalem, as is contained in the book of Enoch the righteous

XI. 1–XII. 7. Levi's Sons and Grand-children

XI. Therefore when I took a wife I was twenty-eight years old, and her name was Melcha. 2. And she conceived and bare a son, and I called his name Gersam, for we were sojourners in our land. 3. And I saw concerning him, that he would not be in the first rank. 4 And Kohath was born in the thirty-fifth year ⌐of my life¬, towards sunrise. 5. And I saw in a vision that he was standing on high in the midst of all the congregation. 6. Therefore I called his name Kohath [which is, beginning of majesty and instruction]. 7. And she bare me a third son, Merari, in the fortieth year of my life; and since his mother bare him with difficulty, I called him Merari, that is my bitterness, because he also was like to die. 8. And Jochebed was born in Egypt, in my sixty-fourth year, for I was renowned then in the midst of my brethren

XII. And Gersam took a wife, and she bare to him Lomni and Semei. 2. And the sons of Kohath, Ambram, Issachar, Hebron, and Ozeel. 3. And the sons of Merari, Mooli and Mouses. 4. And ⌐in my ninety-fourth year¬ Ambram took Jochebed my daughter to him to wife, for they were born in one day, he and my daughter. 5. Eight years old was I when I went into the land of Canaan, and eighteen years when I slew Shechem, and at nineteen years

I became priest, and at twenty-eight years I took a
wife, and at forty-eight I went into Egypt 6 And
behold, my children, ye are a third generation   7.
In my hundred-and-eighteenth year Joseph died.

XIII 1-9 Levi's Instruction to his Children

XIII. And now, my children, I command you :
Fear the Lord your God ⌜with your whole heart⌝,
And walk in simplicity according to all His
law

2. And do ye also teach your children letters,
That they may have understanding all their life,
Reading unceasingly the law of God

3. For every one that knoweth the law of the Lord
shall be honoured,
And shall not be a stranger whithersoever he
goeth

4 Yea, many friends shall he gain more than his
parents,
And many men shall desire to serve him,
And to hear the law from his mouth.

5. Work righteousness, ⌜therefore,⌝ my children,
upon the earth,
That ye may have (it) as a treasure in heaven

6. And sow good things in your souls,
That ye may find them in your life.
But if ye sow evil things,
Ye shall reap every trouble and affliction

7 Get wisdom in the fear of God with diligence ;
For though there be a leading into captivity,
And cities and lands be destroyed,
And gold and silver and every possession perish,
The wisdom of the wise naught can take away,
Save the blindness of ungodliness, and the cal-
lousness (that comes) of sin.

8 ⌜For if one keep oneself from these evil things,⌝
Then even among his enemies shall wisdom be a
glory to him,
And in a strange country a fatherland,
And in the midst of foes shall prove a friend

9. Whosoever teacheth noble things and doeth them,
Shall be enthroned with kings,
As was also Joseph my brother.

XIV. 1–XVI. 5.   Levi foretells the Falling-away of his Children

XIV. Therefore, my children, I have learnt that at the end of the ages ye will transgress against the Lord, stretching out hands to wickedness [against Him]; and to all the Gentiles shall ye become a scorn. 2 For our father Israel is pure from the transgressions of the chief priests [who shall lay their hands upon the Saviour of the world]. 3. For as the heaven is purer in the Lord's sight than the earth, so also be ye, the lights of Israel, (purer) than all the Gentiles. 4 But if ye be darkened through transgressions, what, therefore, will all the Gentiles do living in blindness? Yea, ye shall bring a curse upon our race, because the light of the law which was given for to lighten every man, this ye desire to destroy by teaching commandments contrary to the ordinances of God. 5. The offerings of the Lord ye shall rob, and from His portion shall ye steal choice portions, eating (them) contemptuously with harlots. 6. And out of covetousness ye shall teach the commandments of the Lord, wedded women shall ye pollute, ⌐and the virgins of Jerusalem shall ye defile⌐, and with harlots and adulteresses shall ye be joined, and the daughters of the Gentiles shall ye take to wife, purifying them with an unlawful purification; and your union shall be like unto Sodom and Gomorrah. 7. And ye shall be puffed up because of your priesthood, lifting yourselves up against men, and not only so, but also against the commands of God. 8. For ye shall contemn the holy things with jests and laughter.

XV. Therefore the temple, which the Lord shall choose, shall be laid waste through your uncleanness, and ye shall be captives throughout all nations. 2. And ye shall be an abomination unto them, and ye shall receive reproach and everlasting shame from the righteous judgement of God. 3. And all who hate you shall rejoice at your destruction. 4 And if you were not to receive mercy through Abraham, Isaac, and Jacob, our fathers, not one of our seed should be left upon the earth.

XVI And now I have learnt that for seventy weeks ye shall go astray, and profane the priesthood, and pollute the sacrifices. 2. And ye shall make void the law, and set at nought the words of the prophets by evil perverseness. And ye shall persecute righteous men, and hate the godly; the words of the faithful shall ye abhor. 3 [And a man who reneweth the law in the power of the Most High, ye shall call a deceiver; and at last ye shall rush (upon him) to slay him, not knowing his dignity, taking innocent blood through wickedness upon your heads] 4 And your holy places shall be laid waste even to the ground because of him. 5. And ye shall have no place that is clean; but ye shall be among the Gentiles a curse and a dispersion until He shall again visit you, and in pity shall receive you [through faith and water].

XVII. 1–11. A Decadent Priesthood

XVII. And whereas ye have heard concerning the seventy weeks, hear also concerning the priesthood. 2. For in each jubilee there shall be a priesthood And in the first jubilee, the first who is anointed to the priesthood shall be great, and shall speak to God as to a father. And his priesthood shall be perfect with the Lord, [and in the day of his gladness shall he arise for the salvation of the world] 3. In the second jubilee, he that is anointed shall be conceived in the sorrow of beloved ones; and his priesthood shall be honoured and shall be glorified by all. 4 And the third priest shall be taken hold of by sorrow. 5. And the fourth shall be in pain, because unrighteousness shall gather itself against him exceedingly, and all Israel shall hate each one his neighbour.

6. The fifth shall be taken hold of by darkness 7. Likewise also the sixth and the seventh 8. And in the seventh shall be such pollution as I cannot express before men, for they shall know it who do these things 9 Therefore shall they be taken captive and become a prey, and their land and their substance shall be destroyed

10 And in the fifth week they shall return to their desolate country, and shall renew the house of the Lord 11. And in the seventh week shall come priests, (who are) idolaters, adulterers, lovers of money, proud, lawless, lascivious, abusers of children and beasts.

XVIII. 1–14. A Messianic Hymn

XVIII And after their punishment shall have come from the Lord, the priesthood shall fail

2 Then shall the Lord raise up a new priest
    And to him all the words of the Lord shall be
        revealed ;
    And he shall execute a righteous judgement upon
        the earth for a multitude of days.
3 And his star shall arise in heaven as of a king,
    Lighting up the light of knowledge as the sun
        the day,
    And he shall be magnified in the world
4 He shall shine forth as the sun on the earth,
    And shall remove all darkness from under
        heaven,
    And there shall be peace in all the earth.
5. The heavens shall exult in his days,
    And the earth shall be glad,
    And the clouds shall rejoice ;
    [And the knowledge of the Lord shall be poured
        forth upon the earth, as the water of the seas ;]
    And the angels of the glory of the presence of
        the Lord shall be glad in him.
6. The heavens shall be opened,
    And from the temple of glory shall come upon
        him sanctification,

With the Father's voice as from Abraham to
Isaac.

7. And the glory of the Most High shall be uttered
over him,
And the spirit of understanding and sanctifi-
cation shall rest upon him [in the water].

8 For he shall give the majesty of the Lord to
His sons in truth for evermore ;
And there shall none succeed him for all gener-
ations for ever

9 And in his priesthood the Gentiles shall be
multiplied in knowledge upon the earth,
And enlightened through the grace of the Lord :
In his priesthood shall sin come to an end,
And the lawless shall cease to do evil.
[And the just shall rest in him]

10 And he shall open the gates of paradise,
And shall remove the threatening sword against
Adam.

11 And he shall give to the saints to eat from the
tree of life,
And the spirit of holiness shall be on them.

12 And Beliar shall be bound by him,.
And he shall give power to His children to
tread upon the evil spirits.

13. And the Lord shall rejoice in His children,
And be well pleased in His beloved ones for
ever.

14. Then shall Abraham and Isaac and Jacob exult,
And I will be glad,
And all the saints shall clothe themselves with
joy.

XIX. 1–5   Levi's Last Words to his Children. His Death and Burial

XIX. And now, my children, ye have heard all ;
choose, therefore, for yourselves either the light or
the darkness, either the law of the Lord or the works
of Beliar. 2 And his sons answered him, saying,
Before the Lord we will walk according to His law.

3. And their father said unto them, The Lord is witness, and His angels are witnesses, and ye are witnesses, and I am witness, concerning the word of your mouth. And his sons said unto him : We are witnesses. 4. And thus Levi ceased commanding his sons; and he stretched out his feet ⌜on the bed⌝, and was gathered to his fathers, after he had lived a hundred and thirty-seven years. 5. And they laid him in a coffin, and afterwards they buried him in Hebron, with Abraham, Isaac, and Jacob.

THE TESTAMENT OF JUDAH, THE FOURTH SON OF JACOB AND LEAH

I. 1–VIII. 3.   Judah's Mighty Deeds

I THE copy of the words of Judah, what things he spake to his sons before he died. 2 They gathered themselves together, therefore, and came to him, and he said to them : 3. ⌜Hearken, my children, to Judah your father.⌝ I was the fourth son born to my father Jacob; and Leah my mother named me Judah, saying, I give thanks to the Lord, because He hath given me a fourth son ⌜also⌝. 4. I was swift in my youth, and obedient to my father in everything. 5. And I honoured my mother and my mother's sister. 6. And it came to pass, when I became a man, that my father blessed me, saying, Thou shalt be a king, prospering in all things.

II. And the Lord showed me favour in all my works both in the field and in the house. 2. I know that I raced a hind, and caught it, and prepared the meat for my father, and he did eat. 3. And the roes I used to master in the chase, and overtake all that was in the plains. A wild mare I overtook, and caught it and tamed it. 4. I slew a lion and plucked a kid out of its mouth. I took a bear by its paw and hurled it down the cliff, and it was crushed.

5. I outran the wild boar, and seizing it ⌐as I ran⌐,
I tare it in sunder. 6. A leopard in Hebron leaped
upon my dog, and I caught it by the tail, and hurled
it on the rocks, and it was broken in twain. 7. I
found a wild ox feeding in the fields, and seizing
it by the horns, and whirling it round and stunning
it, I cast it from me and slew it

III. And when the two kings of the Canaanites
came, sheathed in armour, against our flocks, and
much people with them, single-handed I rushed upon
the king of Hazor, and smote him on the greaves and
dragged him down, and so I slew him   2. And the
other, the king of Tappuah, as he sat upon his horse,
[I slew, and so I scattered all his people   3. Achor,
the king] a man of giant stature ⌐I found⌐, hurling
javelins before and behind as he sat on horseback,
and I took up a stone of sixty pounds weight, and
hurled it and smote his horse, and killed it.   4. And
I fought with (this) other for two hours, and I clave
his shield in twain, and I chopped off his feet, and
killed him   5. And as I was stripping off his breastplate, behold nine men, his companions, began to
fight with me   6. And I wound my garment on my
hand; and I slung stones at them, and killed four of
them, and the rest fled   7. And Jacob my father
slew Beelesath, king of all the kings, a giant in
strength, twelve cubits high.   8. And fear fell upon
them, and they ceased warring against us   9.
Therefore my father was free from anxiety in the
wars when I was with my brethren   10. For he
saw in a vision ⌐concerning me⌐ that an angel of
might followed me everywhere, that I should not be
overcome.

IV. And in the south there came upon us a greater
war than that in Shechem, and I joined in battle
array with my brethren, and pursued a thousand
men, and slew of them two hundred men and four
kings.   2. And I went up upon the wall, and I slew
four mighty men.   3. And so we captured Hazor,
and took all the spoil

D

V. On the next day we departed to Aretan, a city strong and walled and inaccessible, threatening us with death 2 But I and Gad approached on the east side of the city, and Reuben and Levi on the west. 3 And they that were upon the wall, thinking that we were alone, were drawn down against us. 4. And so my brothers secretly climbed up the wall on both sides by stakes, and entered the city, while the men knew it not. 5 And we took it with the edge of the sword And as for those who had taken refuge in the tower, we set fire to the tower and took both it and them. 6. And as we were departing the men of Tappuah seized our spoil, and seeing (this) we fought with them. 7. And we slew them all and recovered our spoil.

VI. And when I was at the waters of Kozeba, the men of Jobel came against us to battle. 2 And we fought with them and routed them; ⌜and their allies from Shiloh we slew,⌝ and we did not leave them ⌜power⌝ to come in against us 3. And the men of Makir came upon us the fifth day, to seize our spoil; and we attacked them and overcame them in fierce battle : for there was a host of mighty men amongst them, and we slew them before they had gone up the ascent 4. And when we came to their city their women rolled upon us stones from the brow of the hill on which the city stood 5. And I and Simeon hid ourselves behind the town, and seized upon the heights and destroyed this city also

VII. And the next day it was told us that the king of the city of Gaash with a mighty host was coming against us. 2. I, therefore, and Dan feigned ourselves to be Amorites, and as allies went into their city 3 And in the depth of night our brethren came and we opened to them the gates, and we destroyed all the men and their substance, and we took for a prey all that was theirs and their three walls we cast down 4. And we drew near to Thamna, where was all the substance of the hostile kings.

5 Then being insulted by them, I was therefore wroth, and rushed against them to the summit, and they kept slinging against me stones and darts. 6 And had not Dan my brother aided me, they would have slain me 7 We came upon them, therefore, with wrath, and they all fled, and passing by another way, they besought my father, and he made peace with them 8 And we did to them no hurt, and they became tributary to us, and we restored to them their spoil 9 And I built Thamna, and my father built Rabael 10 I was twenty years old when this war befell 11 And the Canaanites feared me and my brethren

VIII And I had much cattle, and I had for chief herdsman Iram the Adullamite 2 And when I went to him I saw Barsaba, king of Adullam, ⌐and he spake unto us,¬ and he made us a feast, and when I was heated he gave me his daughter Bathshua to wife 3 She bare me Er, and Onan, and Shelah; and two of them the Lord smote for Shelah lived, and his children are ye.

IX 1-8. The Conflict between Jacob and Esau

IX And eighteen years my father abode at peace with his brother Esau, and his sons with us, after that we came from Mesopotamia, from Laban 2 And when eighteen years were fulfilled, in the fortieth year of my life, Esau, the brother of my father, came upon us with a mighty and strong people 3 And Jacob smote Esau with an arrow, and he was taken up wounded on Mount Seir, and as he went he died at Anoniram 4. And we pursued after the sons of Esau Now they had a city with walls of iron and gates of brass; and we could not enter ⌐into it¬, and we encamped around, and besieged it 5. And when they opened not to us in twenty days, I set up a ladder ⌐in the sight of all¬, and with my shield upon my head I went up, sustaining the assaults of stones, upwards of three talents weight; and I

slew four of their mighty men 6. And Reuben and
Gad slew six others   7. Then they asked from us
terms of peace; and having taken counsel with our
father, we received them as tributaries.   8. And they
gave us five hundred cors of wheat, five hundred
baths of oil, five hundred measures of wine, ⌜until
the famine,⌝ when we went down into Egypt.

X. 1–XII. 12. The Story of Tamar

X And after these things my son Er took to
wife Tamar, from Mesopotamia, a daughter of Aram.
2. Now Er was wicked, and he was in need concerning
Tamar, because she was not of the land of Canaan.
And on the third night an angel of the Lord smote
him   3 ⌜And he had not known her according to
the evil craftiness of his mother, for he did not wish
to have children by her   4 In the days⌝ of the
wedding-feast I gave Onan to her in marriage; and
he also in wickedness knew her not, though he spent
with her a year.   5 And when I threatened him he
went in unto her, but he spilled the seed on the
ground, according to the command of his mother,
and he also died through wickedness   6. And I
wished to give Shelah also to her, but his mother
did not permit it, ⌜for she wrought evil against
Tamar,⌝ because she was not of the daughters of
Canaan, as she also herself was.

XI. And I knew that the race of the Canaanites
was wicked, but the impulse of youth blinded my
mind   2 And when I saw her pouring out wine,
owing to the intoxication of wine was I deceived,
and took her although my father had not counselled
(it)   3. And while I was away she went and took
for Shelah a wife from Canaan.   4 And when I knew
what she had done, I cursed her in the anguish of my
soul.   5 And she also died through her wickedness
together with her sons

XII. And after these things, while Tamar was a
widow, she heard after two years that I was going
up to shear my sheep, and adorned herself in bridal

array, and sat in the city Enaim by the gate ⌐2.
For it was a law of the Amorites, that she who was
about to marry should sit in fornication seven days
by the gate ⌐ 3 Therefore being drunk with wine,
I did not recognise her, and her beauty deceived
me, through the fashion of her adorning 4. And
I turned aside to her, and said Let me go in unto
thee. And she said What wilt thou give me?
And I gave her my staff, and my girdle, and the
diadem of my kingdom ⌐in pledge ⌐ And I went in
unto her, and she conceived 5 And not knowing
what I had done, wished to slay her; but she privily
sent my pledges, and put me to shame 6 And
when I called her, I heard also the secret words
which ⌐I spoke⌐ when lying with her in my drunkenness; and I could not slay her, because it was from
the Lord 7 For I said, Lest haply she did it in
subtlety, having received the pledge from another
woman 8 But I came not again near her while
I lived, because I had done ⌐this⌐ abomination in
⌐all⌐ Israel. 9 Moreover, they who were in the
city said that there was no harlot in the gate, because
she came from another place, and sat for a while
in the gate. 10. And I thought that no one knew that
I had gone in to her 11 And after this we came
into Egypt ⌐to Joseph⌐, because of the famine 12
And I was forty and six years old, and seventy and
three years lived I in Egypt

XIII 1–XIX 4 Judah warns his Sons against Drunkenness, Fornication, and the Love of Money

XIII. And now I command you, my children,
hearken ⌐to Judah your father,⌐ and keep my sayings
to perform all the ordinances of the Lord, and to
obey the commands of God 2. And walk not after
your lusts, nor in the imaginations of your thoughts
in haughtiness of heart; and glory not in the deeds
and strength of your youth, for this also is evil in
the eyes of the Lord 3. Since I also gloried that

in wars no comely woman's face ever enticed me,
and reproved Reuben my brother concerning Bilhah,
the wife of my father, the spirits of jealousy and of
fornication arrayed themselves against me, until I
lay with Bathshua the Canaanite, and Tamar, who
was espoused to my sons.   4. For I said to my father-
in-law   I will take counsel with my father, and so
will I take thy daughter   And he was unwilling, but
he showed me a boundless store of gold in his daughter's behalf; for he was a king.   5 And he adorned
her with gold and pearls, and caused her to pour out
wine for us at the feast with the beauty of women.
6 And the wine turned aside my eyes, and pleasure
blinded my heart   7 And I became enamoured of
and I lay with her, and transgressed the commandment of the Lord and the commandment of my
fathers, and I took her to wife.   8. And the Lord
rewarded me according to the imagination of my
heart, inasmuch as I had no joy in her children.

XIV. And now, my children, ⌈I say unto you,⌉
be not drunk with wine; for wine turneth the mind
away from the truth, and inspires the passion of
lust, and leadeth the eyes into error.   2. For the
spirit of fornication hath wine as a minister to give
pleasure to the mind, for these two also take away
the mind of man.   3 For if a man drink wine to
drunkenness, it disturbeth the mind with filthy
thoughts ⌈leading to fornication⌉, and heateth the
body to carnal union; and if the occasion of the lust
be present, he worketh the sin, and is not ashamed
4 Such is the inebriated man, my children, for he
who is drunken reverenceth no man.   5 For, lo, it
made me also to err, so that I was not ashamed of
the multitude in the city, in that before the eyes of all
I turned aside unto Tamar, and I wrought a great
sin, and I uncovered the covering of my sons'
shame.   6. After I had drunk wine I reverenced not
the commandment of God, and I took a woman of
Canaan to wife.   7. For much discretion needeth
the man who drinketh wine, my children; and herein

is discretion in drinking wine, a man may drink so long as he preserveth modesty. 8. But if he go beyond this limit the spirit of deceit attacketh his mind, and it maketh the drunkard to talk filthily, and to transgress and not to be ashamed, but even to glory in his shame, and account himself honourable.

XV. He that committeth fornication is not aware when he suffers loss, and is not ashamed when put to dishonour 2. For even though a man be a king and commit fornication, he is stripped of his kingship by becoming the slave of fornication, as I myself also suffered 3. For I gave my staff, that is, the stay of my tribe; and my girdle, that is, my power, and my diadem, that is, the glory of my kingdom 4. And indeed I repented of these things; wine and flesh I eat not until my old age, nor did I behold any joy 5. And the angel of God showed me that for ever do women bear rule over king and beggar alike. 6. And from the king they take away his glory, and from the valiant man his might, and from the beggar even that little which is the stay of his poverty

XVI. Observe, therefore, my children, the (right) limit in wine, for there are in it four evil spirits—of lust, of hot desire, of profligacy, of filthy lucre 2. If ye drink wine in gladness, be ye modest with the fear of God For if in (your) gladness the fear of God departeth, then drunkenness ariseth and shamelessness stealeth in 3. But if you would live soberly do not touch wine at all, lest ye sin in words of outrage, and in fightings and slanders, and transgressions of the commandments of God, and ye perish before your time 4. Moreover, wine revealeth the mysteries of God and men, even as I also revealed the commandments of God and the mysteries of Jacob my father to the Canaanitish woman Bathshua, which God bade me not to reveal 5. And wine is a cause both of war and confusion.

XVII. And now I command you, my children, not to love money, nor to gaze upon the beauty of women, because for the sake of money and beauty

I was led astray to Bathshua the Canaanite. [2.
For I know that because of these two things shall my
race fall into wickedness. 3 For even wise men
among my sons shall they mar, and shall cause the
kingdom of Judah to be diminished, which the Lord
gave me because of my obedience to my father. 4
For I never caused grief to Jacob, my father; for
all things whatsoever he commanded I did. 5 And
Isaac, the father of my father, blessed me to be king
in Israel, and Jacob further blessed me in like manner.
6. And I know that from me shall the kingdom be
established.

XVIII And I know what evils ye will do in the
last days.]

    2. Beware, therefore, my children, of fornication
        and the love of money, and hearken to Judah
        your father.

    3 For these things withdraw you from the law of
        God,
        And blind the inclination of the soul,
        And teach arrogance,
        And suffer not a man to have compassion upon
        his neighbour.

    4. They rob his soul of all goodness,
        And oppress him with toils and troubles,
        ⌜And drive away sleep from him,⌝
        And devour his flesh.

    5 And he hindereth the sacrifices of God;
        ⌜And he remembereth not the blessing of God,⌝
        He hearkeneth not to a prophet when he speaketh,
        And resenteth the words of godliness.

    ⌜6 For he is a slave to two contrary passions,
        And cannot obey God,
        Because they have blinded his soul,
        And he walketh in the day as in the night.⌝

XIX. My children, the love of money leadeth to
idolatry; because, when led astray through money,
men name as gods those who are not gods, and it
causeth him who hath it to fall into madness. 2
For the sake of money I lost my children, and had

not my repentance, ⌐and my humiliation,⌐ and the
prayers of my father been accepted, I should have
died childless 3 But the God of my fathers had
mercy on me, because I did it in ignorance. 4 And
the prince of deceit blinded me, and I was ignorant
as a man and as flesh, being corrupted through sins ;
⌐and I learnt my own weakness while thinking myself
invincible⌐.

XX. 1–5. The Spirits that wait upon Man

XX. Know, therefore, my children, that two
spirits wait upon man—the spirit of truth and the
spirit of deceit 2 And in the midst is the spirit
of the understanding of the mind, to which it belongeth to turn whithersoever it will 3 And the works
of truth and the works of deceit are written upon the
hearts of men, and each one of them the Lord
knoweth 4 And there is no time at which the
works of men can be hid ; for on the heart itself have
they been written down ⌐before the Lord⌐ 5 And
the spirit of truth testifieth all things, and accuseth
all, and the sinner is burnt up ⌐by his own heart⌐,
and cannot raise his face ⌐to the judge⌐

XXI. 1–5 The Levitical Priesthood and the Kingdom of Judah

XXI And now, my children, I command you, love
Levi, that ye may abide, and ⌐exalt not yourselves
against him⌐, lest ye be utterly destroyed 2 ⌐For
to me the Lord gave the kingdom, and to him the
priesthood, and He set the kingdom beneath the
priesthood 3 To me He gave the things upon the
earth ; to him the things in the heavens 4 As the
heaven is higher than the earth, so is the priesthood
of God higher than the earthly kingdom, unless it
falleth away through sin from the Lord and is domin-
ated by the earthly kingdom ⌐ 5 For ⌐the angel
of the Lord said unto me⌐ · The Lord chose him rather
than thee, to draw near to Him, and to eat of His
table ⌐and to offer Him the first-fruits⌐ of the choice

things of the sons of Israel; but thou shalt be king of Jacob.

XXI. 6-XXII. 3. Turmoil in the Last Times

6. And thou shalt be amongst them as the sea. For as, on the sea, just and unjust are tossed about, ⸀some taken into captivity while some are enriched,⸀ so also shall every race of men be in thee : some shall be impoverished, being taken captive, ⸀and others grow rich by plundering the possessions of others⸀.

7. For the kings shall be as sea-monsters.
They shall swallow men like fishes :
The sons and daughters ⸀of freemen⸀ shall they enslave ;
Houses, lands, flocks, money shall they plunder :

8. And with the flesh of many shall they ⸀wrongfully⸀ feed the ravens and the cranes ;
⸀And they shall advance in evil, in covetousness uplifted,⸀

9. And there shall be false prophets ⸀like⸀ tempests,
And they shall persecute all righteous men

XXII. And the Lord shall bring upon them divisions ⸀one against another⸀.
And there shall be ⸀continual⸀ wars in Israel ;

2. And among men of another race shall my kingdom be brought to an end,
Until the salvation of Israel shall come,
⸀Until the appearing of the God of righteousness⸀,
That Jacob [and all the Gentiles] may rest in peace

3. And He shall guard the might of my kingdom for ever ;
For the Lord sware to me with an oath that He would not destroy the kingdom from my seed for ever.

XXIII. 1-XXV. 5. The Sins of Israel ; Regeneration in the Messianic Era

XXIII Now I have much grief, my children, because of your lewdness and witchcrafts, and idola-

tries which ye shall practise ⌈against the kingdom⌉,
following them that have familiar spirits, diviners,
and demons of error. 2. Ye shall make your daughters singing girls and harlots, and ye shall mingle
in the abominations of the Gentiles 3 For which
things' sake the Lord shall bring upon you famine
and pestilence, death and the sword, beleaguering
by enemies, and revilings of friends, the slaughter of
children, the rape of wives, the plundering of possessions, [the burning of the temple of God,] the laying
waste of the land, the enslavement of yourselves
among the Gentiles 4 And they shall make some
of you eunuchs for their wives. 5 Until the Lord
visit you, when with perfect heart ye repent and
walk in all His commandments, and He bring you up
from captivity among the Gentiles

XXIV. And after these things shall a star arise to
you from Jacob in peace,
> And a man shall arise [from my seed], like the
> sun of righteousness,
> Walking with the sons of men in meekness and
> righteousness,
> And no sin shall be found in him.

2 And the heavens shall be opened unto him,
> To pour out the spirit, (even) the blessing of the
> Holy Father;

3 And He shall pour out the spirit of grace upon
> you,
> And ye shall be unto Him sons in truth,
> And ye shall walk in His commandments first
> and last

4 [This Branch of God Most High,
> And this Fountain giving life unto all]

5. Then shall the sceptre of my kingdom shine
> forth;
> And from your root shall arise a stem,

6 And from it shall grow a rod of righteousness to
> the Gentiles,
> To judge and to save all that call upon the
> Lord.

XXV. And after these things shall Abraham and Isaac and Jacob arise unto life, and I and my brethren shall be chiefs of the tribes ⌜of Israel⌝ : Levi first, I the second, Joseph third, Benjamin fourth, Simeon fifth, Issachar sixth, and so all in order. 2. And the Lord blessed Levi, and the Angel of the Presence, me , the powers of glory, Simeon ; the heaven, Reuben ; the earth, Issachar ; the sea, Zebulun ; the mountains, Joseph ; the tabernacle, Benjamin ; the luminaries, Dan ; Eden, Naphtali ; the sun, Gad ; the moon, Asher.

3 And ye shall be the people of the Lord, and have one tongue ;

And there shall be there no spirit of deceit of ⌜Beliar⌝,

For he shall be cast into the fire for ever

4 And they who have died in grief shall arise ⌜in joy⌝,

⌜And they who were poor for the Lord's sake shall be made rich,⌝

And they who are put to death for the Lord's sake shall awake ⌜to life⌝

5 And the harts of Jacob shall run ⌜in joyfulness⌝,

And the eagles of Israel shall fly ⌜in gladness⌝,

And all the peoples shall glorify the Lord for ever

XXVI. 1-4. Judah's Last Words to his Sons. His Death and Burial

XXVI Observe, therefore, my children, all the law of the Lord, for there is hope for all them who hold fast unto His ways 2 And ⌜he said to them : Behold,⌝ I die before your eyes this day, a hundred and nineteen years old. 3 Let no one bury me ⌜in costly apparel⌝, nor tear open my bowels, ⌜for this shall they who are kings do ,⌝ and carry me up to Hebron with you. 4. And Judah, when he had said these things, fell asleep ; and his sons did according to all whatsoever he commanded them, and they buried him in Hebron with his fathers.

THE TESTAMENT OF ISSACHAR, THE FIFTH
SON OF JACOB AND LEAH

I 1–II 5. Introduction. The Dissension between Rachel and Leah

I THE copy of the words of Issachar. For he called his sons and said to them :

Hearken, my children, to Issachar your father ;
Give ear to the words of him who is beloved of the Lord

2 I was born the ⌜fifth son to Jacob⌝, by way of hire for the mandrakes 3. For Reuben ⌜my brother⌝ brought in mandrakes from the field, and Rachel met him and took them. 4. And Reuben wept, and at his voice Leah my mother came forth 5 Now these (mandrakes) were ⌜sweet-smelling⌝ apples which were produced in the land of Haran below a ravine of water 6 And Rachel said : I will not give them to thee, but they shall be to me instead of children ⌜For the Lord hath despised me, and I have not borne children to Jacob⌝ 7. Now there were two apples ; and Leah said ⌜to Rachel⌝ : Let it suffice thee that thou hast taken my husband wilt thou take these also ? 8 And Rachel said ⌜to her⌝ : Thou shalt have Jacob this night for the mandrakes ⌜of thy son⌝. 9 And Leah said to her . Jacob is mine, for I am the wife of his youth 10 But Rachel said · Boast not, and vaunt not thyself, for he espoused me before thee, and for my sake he served our father fourteen years. 11 And had not craft increased on the earth and the wickedness of men prospered, thou wouldest not now see the face of Jacob 12. For thou art not his wife, but in craft wert taken to him in my stead. 13 And my father deceived me, ⌜and removed me on that night⌝, and did not suffer ⌜Jacob to see me ; for⌝ had I been there, this had not happened ⌜to him⌝ 14 Nevertheless, for the mandrakes I am hiring Jacob to

thee for one night.   15. And Jacob knew Leah, and she ⌈conceived and⌉ bare me, and on account of the hire I was called Issachar.

II   Then appeared to Jacob an angel of the Lord, saying   Two children shall Rachel bear, inasmuch as she hath refused company with her husband, and hath chosen continency.   2. And had not Leah my mother paid the two apples for the sake of his company, she would have borne eight sons, for this reason she bare six, and Rachel bare the two : for on account of the mandrakes the Lord visited her. 3. For He knew that for the sake of children she wished to company with Jacob, and not for lust of pleasure   4 For on the morrow also she again gave up Jacob   Because of the mandrakes, therefore, the Lord hearkened to Rachel   5 For though she desired them, she ate them not, but offered them in the house of the Lord, presenting them to the priest of the Most High who was at that time

III. 1–V. 8.   Issachar's Exhortation to his Sons

III. When, therefore, I grew up, my children, I walked in uprightness of heart, and I became a husbandman for my father and my brethren, and I brought in fruits from the field according to their season   2 ⌈And my father blessed me, for he saw that I walked in rectitude before him⌉   3. And I was not a busybody in my doings, ⌈nor envious and malicious against my neighbour.   4 I never slandered any one, nor did I censure, the life of any man, walking as I did in singleness of eye⌉   5 Therefore, when I was thirty-⌈five⌉ years old, I took to myself a wife, for my labour wore away my strength, and I never thought upon pleasure with women, but owing to my toil, sleep overcame me   6. And my father ⌈always⌉ rejoiced in my rectitude, ⌈because I offered through the priest to the Lord all first-fruits; then to my father also   7 And the Lord increased ten thousandfold His benefits in my hands, and also Jacob, my father, knew that God aided my

singleness 8. For on all the poor and oppressed I
bestowed the good things of the earth in the singleness of my heart⌐

IV And now, hearken to me, my children,
And walk in singleness ⌐of your heart⌐,
For I have seen in it ⌐all⌐ that is well-pleasing
to the Lord

2 ⌐The single-(minded) man coveteth not gold,
He overreacheth not his neighbour,
He longeth not after manifold dainties,
He delighteth not in varied apparel.

3 He doth not desire to live a long life,
But only waiteth for the will of God ⌐

4 And the spirits of deceit have no power against
him,
For he looketh not on the beauty of women,
⌐Lest he should pollute his mind with corrup-
tion⌐

5 There is no envy in his thoughts,
[Nor malicious person maketh his soul to pine
away,]
Nor worry with insatiable desire in his mind

6 For he walketh in singleness ⌐of soul⌐,
And beholdeth all things in uprightness ⌐of
heart⌐,
Shunning eyes (made) evil through the error of
the world,
Lest he should see the perversion of any of the
commandments of the Lord

V. Keep, therefore, my children, the law of God,
And get singleness,
⌐And walk in guilelessness,
Not playing the busybody with the business of
your neighbour

2 But love the Lord and your neighbour,
Have compassion on the poor and weak.⌐

3 Bow down your back unto husbandry,
And toil in labours ⌐in all manner of husbandry,
Offering gifts to the Lord with thanksgiving⌐

4 For with the first-fruits of the earth will the

Lord bless you, ⌐even as He blessed all the saints
from Abel even until now⌐. 5. For no other portion
is given to you ⌐than of the fatness of the earth,
whose fruits are raised by toil⌐ 6 For our father
Jacob blessed me with blessings of the earth and of
first-fruits. 7. And Levi and Judah were glorified
by the Lord even among the sons of Jacob, for the
Lord gave them an inheritance, and to Levi He gave
the priesthood, and to Judah the kingdom 8 And
do ye therefore obey them, and walk in the singleness
of your father; [for unto Gad hath it been given to
destroy the troops that are coming upon Israel]

VI 1–3. Iniquity in the Last Times

VI Know ye, therefore, my children, that in the
   last times
   Your sons will forsake singleness,
   ⌐And will cleave unto insatiable desire,
   And⌐ leaving ⌐guilelessness, will draw near to
      malice;
   And forsaking the commandments of the Lord,
   They will cleave unto Beliar;
2. And leaving⌐ husbandry,
   They will follow after their own ⌐wicked⌐
      devices,
   And they shall be dispersed among the Gentiles,
   And shall serve their enemies
3 And do ye therefore give these commands to
your children, that, if they sin, they may the more
quickly return to the Lord; 4 For He is merciful,
and will deliver them, even to bring them back into
their land.

VII. 1–7 Issachar's Blamelessness

VII. Behold, therefore, as ye see, I am a hundred
and twenty-six years old and am not conscious of
committing any sin. 2. Except my wife I have not
known any woman I never committed fornication
by the uplifting of my ⌐eyes⌐.
   3. I drank not wine, to be led astray thereby;

I coveted not any desirable thing that was my
    neighbour's.

4 Guile arose not in my heart;
    A lie passed not through my lips.

5 If any man were in distress I joined my sighs
    with his,
    And I shared my bread with the poor.
    I wrought godliness, all my days I kept truth.

6. I loved the Lord,
    Likewise also every man with all my heart.

7 So do ye also these things, my children,
    And every spirit of Beliar shall flee from you,
    And no deed of wicked men shall rule over you;
    And every wild beast shall ye subdue,
    Since ye have with you the God of heaven and
    earth
    (And) walk with men in singleness of heart.⌐

VII 8-9   Issachar's Death and Burial

8 And having said these things, he commanded his
sons that they should carry him up to Hebron, and
bury him there in the cave ⌐with his fathers⌐. 9. And
he stretched out his feet and died, the fifth son of
Jacob, at a good old age; with every limb sound,
and with strength unabated, he slept the eternal
sleep

THE TESTAMENT OF ZEBULUN, THE SIXTH
SON OF JACOB AND LEAH

I. 1-IV 13   Introduction. Zebulun's Account
of the Selling of Joseph

I. THE copy of the words of Zebulun, which he
enjoined on his sons ⌐before he died⌐ in the hundred
and fourteenth year of his life, two years after the
death of Joseph 2. And he said to them: Hearken
to me, ye sons of Zebulun, attend to the words of
E

your father   3 I, Zebulun, was born a good gift
to my parents   For when I was born my father was
increased very exceedingly, both in flocks and herds,
when with the straked rods he had his portion   4. I
am not conscious that I have sinned all my days,
ꜣsave in thoughtꜟ   5 Nor yet do I remember that
I have done any iniquity, except the sin of ignorance
which I committed against Joseph, for I covenanted
with my brethren not to tell my father what had been
done   6 But I wept ꜛin secretꜟ many days on
account of Joseph, for I feared my brethren, ꜛbecause
they had all agreed, that if any one should declare
the secret, he should be slainꜟ. 7 But when they
wished to kill him, I adjured them much ꜛwith tearsꜟ
not to be guilty of this sin.

II For Simeon and Gad came against Joseph ꜛto
kill himꜟ, and he said unto them with tears . 2 Pity
me, my brethren, have mercy upon the bowels of
Jacob our father ꞉ lay not upon me your hands ꜛto
shed innocent bloodꜟ, for I have not sinned against
you   3 And if indeed I have sinned, with chastening
chastise me, ꜛmy brethrenꜟ, but lay not upon me
your hand, for the sake of Jacob our father   4. And
as he spoke these words, ꜛwailing as he did soꜟ, I
was unable to bear his lamentatioms, and ꜛbegan to
weepꜟ, and my liver was poured out, and all the
substance of my bowels was loosened. 5 And I
wept with Joseph, and my heart sounded, ꜛand the
joints of my body trembledꜟ, and I was not able to
stand   6 And when ꜛJosephꜟ saw me weeping with
him, and them coming against him to slay him,
he fled behind me, beseeching them   7. But mean-
while Reuben rose and said ꜛCome,ꜟ my brethren, let
us not slay him, but let us cast him into one of these
dry pits, which our fathers digged and found no water.
8 For for this cause the Lord forbade that water
should rise up in them, in order that Joseph should be
preserved   9 And they did so, until they sold him
to the Ishmaelites

III For in his price I had no share, my children

2. But Simeon and Gad and six other of our brethren took the price of Joseph, and bought sandals for themselves, and their wives, ⌜and their children⌝, saying . 3 We will not eat of it, for it is the price of our brother's blood, but we will assuredly tread it under foot, because he said that he would be king over us, ⌜and so let us see what will become of his dreams⌝. 4 Therefore it is written in the writing of the law of Moses, that whosoever will not raise up seed to his brother, his sandal should be unloosed, and they should spit into his face   5 And the brethren of Joseph wished not that their brother should live, and the Lord loosed from them the sandal which they wore against ⌜Joseph their brother⌝   6 For when they came into Egypt ⌜they were unloosed by the servants of Joseph outside the gate, and so they made obeisance to Joseph after the fashion of King Pharaoh. 7 And⌝ not only did they make obeisance to him, but ⌜were spit upon also, falling down before him forthwith, and so⌝ they were put to shame before the Egyptians   8 For after this the Egyptians heard all the evils that they had done to Joseph.

IV   And after he was sold my brothers sat down to eat and drink   2 But I, through pity for Joseph, did not eat, but watched the pit, since Judah feared lest Simeon, Dan, and Gad should rush off and slay him   3 But when they saw that I did not eat, they set me to watch him, till he was sold to the Ishmaelites 5 And when Reuben came and heard that while he was away (Joseph) had been sold, he rent his garments, (and) mourning, said : How shall I look on the face of my father Jacob ?   6 And he took the money and ran after the merchants, but as he failed to find them he returned grieving. But the merchants had left the broad road and marched through the Troglodytes by a short cut   7. ⌜But Reuben was grieved,⌝ and ate no food that day   Dan therefore came to him and said : 8 Weep not, neither grieve , for we have found what we can say to our father Jacob   9 Let us slay a kid of the goats, and dip in it the coat of Joseph ; and

let us send it to Jacob, saying : Know, is this the coat
of thy son? And they did so. 10. ⌐For they stripped
off from Joseph his coat when they were selling him,
and put upon him the garment of a slave.¬ 11. Now
Simeon took the coat, and would not give it up, ⌐for
he wished to rend it with his sword,¬ as he was angry
that Joseph lived and that he had not slain him.
12. Then we ⌐all¬ rose up and said unto him · If
thou givest not up the coat, we will say ⌐to our father¬
that thou alone didst this evil thing in Israel. 13 And
so he gave it unto them, and they did even as Dan
had said.

V. 1–IX. 4. Zebulun's Exhortation to his Sons

V And now, my children, I bid you to keep the
commands of the Lord, ⌐and to show mercy to your
neighbours, and to have compassion towards all,
not towards men only, but also towards beasts.
2. For, for this thing's sake the Lord blessed me,¬
and when all my brethren were sick, I escaped without sickness, for the Lord knoweth the purposes of
each. 3. Have, therefore, compassion in your hearts,
my children, because even as a man doeth to his
neighbour, even so also will the Lord do to him
4 For the sons of my brethren were sickening and
were dying on account of Joseph, ⌐because they
showed not mercy in their hearts¬; but my sons
were preserved without sickness, as ye know. 5. And
when I was in the land of Canaan, by the sea-coast,
I made a catch of fish for Jacob my father; and
when many were choked in the sea, I continued
unhurt.

VI. I was the first to make a boat to sail upon the
sea, for the Lord gave me understanding ⌐and wisdom
therein¬. 2. And I let down a rudder behind it,
and I stretched a sail upon another upright piece of
wood in the midst. 3 And I sailed therein along the
shores, catching fish for the house of my father until
we came to Egypt.

[4. And through compassion I shared my catch

with every stranger. 5 And if a man were a stranger, or sick, or aged, I boiled the fish, and dressed them well, and offered them to all men, as every man had need, grieving with and having compassion upon them 6 Wherefore also the Lord satisfied me with abundance of fish when catching fish, for he that shareth with his neighbour receiveth manifold more from the Lord] 7 For five years I caught fish, [and gave thereof to every man whom I saw, and sufficed for all the house of my father]. 8 And in the summer I caught fish, and in the winter I kept sheep with my brethren

VII. [Now I will declare unto you what I did I saw a man in distress through nakedness in winter-time, and had compassion upon him, and stole away a garment secretly from my father's house, and gave it to him who was in distress 2 Do ye, therefore, my children, from that which God bestoweth upon you, show compassion and mercy without hesitation to all men, and give to every man with a good heart. 3 And if ye have not the wherewithal to give to him that needeth, have compassion for him in bowels of mercy. 4 I know that my hand found not the wherewithal to give to him that needed, and I walked with him weeping for seven furlongs, and my bowels yearned towards him in compassion.

VIII. Have, therefore, yourselves also, my children, compassion towards every man with mercy, that the Lord also may have compassion and mercy upon you. 2 Because also in the last days God will send His compassion on the earth, and wheresoever He findeth bowels of mercy He dwelleth in him 3 For in the degree in which a man hath compassion upon his neighbours, in the same degree hath the Lord also upon him] 4 And when we went down into Egypt, Joseph bore no malice against us 5 To whom taking heed, do ye also, my children, ⌐approve yourselves without malice, and⌐ love one another, and do not set down in account, each one of you, evil against his brother. 6. For this breaketh unity,

and divideth ⌐all kindred, and troubleth the soul⌐,
and weareth away the countenance

IX Observe, ⌐therefore,⌐ the waters, and know
when they flow together, they sweep along stones,
trees, earth, and other things. 2. But if they are
divided into many streams, the earth swalloweth
them up, and they become of no account 3. So
shall ye also be if ye be divided. 4 Be not ye,
therefore, divided into two heads, for everything
which the Lord made hath but one head, and two
shoulders, two hands, two feet, but all the remaining
members.

IX 5–9   Zebulun's Prophecy concerning his Posterity

5. For I have learnt in the writing of my fathers,
that

Ye shall be divided in Israel,
And ye shall follow two kings,
And shall work every abomination
6. And your enemies shall lead you captive,
And ye shall be evil entreated among the Gentiles,
With many infirmities and tribulations.
7 And after these things ye shall remember the
Lord and repent,
And He shall have mercy upon you, for He is
merciful and compassionate.
And He setteth not down in account evil against
the sons of men,
Because they are flesh, and are deceived through
their own wicked deeds
8. And after these things shall there arise ⌐unto you⌐
the Lord Himself, the light of righteousness,
And ye shall return unto your own land.
And ye shall see Him in Jerusalem, ⌐for His
name's sake⌐
9. And again ⌐through the wickedness of your
works⌐ shall ye provoke Him to anger,
And ye shall be cast away ⌐by Him⌐ unto the
time of consummation

X. 1–7 Zebulun's Last Words to his Sons His Death and Burial

X. And now, my children, grieve not that I am dying, nor be cast down in that I am coming to my end 2. For I shall rise again in the midst of you, ⌐as a ruler in the midst of his sons⌐, and I shall rejoice in the midst of my tribe, as many as shall keep the law of the Lord, ⌐and the commandments of Zebulun their father⌐. 3 But upon the ungodly shall the Lord bring eternal fire, and destroy them throughout all generations 4 But I am now hastening away to my rest, as did also my fathers 5 But do ye fear the Lord ⌐our God with all your strength all the days of your life⌐ 6 And when he had said these things he fell asleep, ⌐at a good old age⌐. And his sons laid him in a ⌐wooden⌐ coffin 7 And afterwards they carried him up and buried him in Hebron, with his fathers

THE TESTAMENT OF DAN, THE SEVENTH SON OF JACOB AND BILHAH

I. 1–IV 7 Dan's Confession. His Warning against harbouring Wrath

I. THE copy of the words of Dan, which he spake to his sons in his last days, in the hundred and twenty-fifth year of his life. 2. For he called together his family, and said Hearken to my words, ye sons of Dan, and give heed to the words ⌐of your father⌐. 3 I have proved in my heart, and in my whole life, that truth with just dealing is good and well-pleasing to God, and that lying and anger are evil, because they teach man all wickedness 4 I confess, therefore, this day to you, my children, that in my heart I resolved on the death of Joseph ⌐my brother⌐, the true and good man [5 And I rejoiced that he was

sold, because his father loved him more than us.]
6 For the spirit of jealousy and vain-glory said to me :
Thou thyself also art his son.   7. And one of the spirits
of Beliar stirred me up, saying : Take this sword, and
⌜with it⌝ slay Joseph ; so shall thy father love thee
when he is dead.   8. Now this was the spirit of
anger that persuaded me to crush Joseph as a leopard
crusheth a kid   9 But the God of my fathers did
not suffer him to fall into my hands, so that I should
find him alone and slay him, and cause a second tribe
to be destroyed in Israel.

II. And now, my children, behold I am dying, and
I tell you of a truth, that unless ye keep yourselves
from the spirit of lying and of anger, and love truth
and long-suffering, ye shall perish.   2. For anger is
blindness, and doth not suffer one to see the face of
any man with truth.   3. For though it be a father or
a mother, ⌜he behaveth towards them as enemies⌝ ;
though it be a brother, he knoweth him not ; though
it be a prophet of the Lord, he disobeyeth him , though
a righteous man, he regardeth him not ; ⌜though a
friend, he doth not acknowledge him⌝   4. For the
spirit of anger encompasseth him with the net of
deceit, and blindeth his eyes, and through lying dark-
eneth his mind, and giveth him its own peculiar vision.
5. And wherewith encompasseth it his eyes ? With
hatred of heart, so as to be envious of his brother.

III. For anger is an evil thing, my children, for it
troubleth even the soul itself.

2 And the body of the angry man it maketh its
own, and over his soul it getteth the mastery, and it
bestoweth upon the body ⌜power that it may work
all⌝ iniquity   3 And when the body doeth all these
things, the soul justifieth what is done, since it seeth
not aright.   4. Therefore he who is wrathful, if he
be a mighty man, hath a threefold power in his anger :
one by the help of his servants ; and a second by his
wealth, whereby he persuadeth and overcometh
wrongfully ; and thirdly, having his own natural
power he worketh thereby the evil.   5. And though

the wrathful man be weak, yet hath he a power
twofold of that which is by nature; for wrath ever
aideth such in lawlessness. 6 This spirit goeth
always with lying ⌐at the right hand of Satan, that
with cruelty and lying⌐ his works may be wrought
    IV. Understand ye, therefore, the power of wrath,
that it is vain   2. For it first of all giveth provocation
by word, then by deeds it strengtheneth him who
is angry, and with sharp losses disturbeth his mind,
and so stirreth up with great wrath his soul   3 Therefore, when any one speaketh against you, be not ye
moved to anger, [and if any man praiseth you as
holy men, be not uplifted : be not moved either to
delight or to disgust]. 4. For first it pleaseth the
hearing, and so maketh the mind keen to perceive the
grounds for provocation, and then being enraged, he
thinketh that he is justly angry
    5 If ye fall into any loss or ruin, my children, ⌐be
not afflicted⌐, for this very spirit maketh (a man)
desire that which is perishable, in order that he may
be enraged through the affliction   6. And if ye suffer
loss voluntarily, or involuntarily, be not vexed, for
from vexation ariseth wrath ⌐with lying⌐. 7. Moreover, a twofold mischief is wrath with lying; and
they assist one another in order to disturb the heart,
and when the soul is continually disturbed, the Lord
departeth from it, and Beliar ruleth over it.

V. 1–3   An Exhortation to keep the Law

V Observe, therefore, my children, the commandments of the Lord,
    And keep His law,
    Depart from wrath,
    And hate lying,
    That the Lord may dwell among you,
    And Beliar may flee from you.
2 Speak truth each one with his neighbour,
    So shall ye not fall into wrath and confusion;
    But ye shall be in peace, having the God of peace,
    So shall no war prevail over you

3 Love the Lord through all your life,
And one another with a true heart.

V. 4–13. The Last Times

4 I know that in the last days ye shall depart
from the Lord,
And ye shall provoke Levi unto anger,
And fight against Judah,
But ye shall not prevail against them,
For an angel of the Lord shall guide them
both;
For by them shall Israel stand

5. And whensoever ye depart from the Lord, ye
shall walk in all evil and work the abominations of
the Gentiles, going a-whoring after women of the
lawless ones, while with all wickedness the spirits of
wickedness work ⌐in you⌐. [6 For I have read in
the book of Enoch, the righteous, that your prince is
Satan, and that all the spirits of wickedness and pride
will conspire to attend constantly on the sons of
Levi, to cause them to sin before the Lord

7. And my sons will draw near to Levi,
And sin with them in all things;
And the sons of Judah will be covetous,
Plundering other men's goods like lions]

8. Therefore shall ye be led away [with them] into
captivity,
And there shall ye receive all the plagues of
Egypt,
And all the evils of the Gentiles

9. And so when ye return to the Lord ye shall
obtain mercy,
And He shall bring you into His sanctuary,
And He shall give you peace

10. And there shall arise unto you from the tribe
of [Judah and of] Levi the salvation of the
Lord;
And he shall make war against Beliar,
And execute an everlasting vengeance on our
enemies;

11. And the captivity shall he take from Beliar
    [the souls of the saints],
    And turn disobedient hearts unto the Lord,
    And give to them that call upon him eternal
    peace.
12. And the saints shall rest in Eden,
    And in the New Jerusalem will the righteous
    rejoice,
    And it shall be unto the glory of God for ever
13. And no longer shall Jerusalem endure desolation,
    Nor Israel be led captive;
    For the Lord shall be in the midst of it [living
    amongst men],
And the Holy One of Israel shall reign over it [in
humility and in poverty, and he who believeth on
Him shall reign amongst men in truth]

VI. 1–11 An Exhortation to Depart from Evil

VI And now, fear the Lord, my children, and
beware of Satan and his spirits. 2 Draw near unto
God and to the angel that intercedeth for you, for he
is a mediator between God and man, and for the peace
of Israel he shall stand up against the kingdom of the
enemy. 3 Therefore is the enemy eager to destroy all
that call upon the Lord. 4 For he knoweth that on
the day on which Israel shall repent, the kingdom of
the enemy shall be brought to an end 5 For the
very angel of peace shall strengthen Israel, that it
fall not into the extremity of evil 6 And it shall
be in the time of the lawlessness of Israel, that the
Lord will (not) depart from them, but will transform
them into a nation that doeth His will, for none of the
angels will be equal unto him 7 And His name
shall be in every place of Israel, ⌐and among the
Gentiles⌐.

8 Keep, therefore, yourselves, my children, from
    every evil work,
    And cast away wrath and all lying,
    And love truth and long-suffering.
9 And the things which ye have heard from your

father, do ye ⌈also⌉ impart to your children [that the
Saviour of the Gentiles may receive you, for he is
true and long-suffering, meek and lowly, and teacheth
by his works the law of God]   10. Depart, therefore, from all unrighteousness, and cleave unto the
righteousness of God, and your race will be saved
for ever.   11 And bury me near my fathers.

VII. 1-3   Dan's Death and Burial

VII. And when he had said these things he kissed
them, and fell asleep at a good old age.   2. And his
sons buried him.   And after that they carried up
⌈his bones⌉, and placed them near Abraham, and
Isaac, and Jacob   3. [Nevertheless, ⌈Dan⌉ prophesied unto them that they should forget their God, and
should be alienated from the land of their inheritance
⌈and from the race of Israel⌉, and from the family
of ⌈their seed ⌉]

THE TESTAMENT OF NAPHTALI, THE EIGHTH
SON OF JACOB AND BILHAH

I. 1-12   Introduction.   Naphtali's Birth

I. THE copy of the testament of Naphtali, which he
ordained at the time of his death in the hundred and
thirtieth year of his life.   2 When his sons were
gathered together in the seventh month, on the first
day of the month, while still in good health, he made
them a feast of food and wine.   3 And after he was
awake in the morning, he said to them, I am dying;
and they believed him not   4 And as he glorified
the Lord, he grew strong and said that after yester-
day's feast he should die.   5. And he began then to
say: Hear, my children, ye sons of Naphtali, hear
the words of your father   6 I was born from ·
Bilhah; ⌈and⌉ because Rachel dealt craftily, and gave

Bilhah in place of herself to Jacob, and she conceived and bare me upon Rachel's knees, ⌐therefore she called my name Naphtali. 7 For Rachel loved me very much because I was born upon her lap⌐, and when I was still young she was wont to kiss me, and say · May I have a brother of thine from mine own womb, like unto thee 8 Whence also Joseph was like unto me ⌐in all things⌐, according to the prayers of Rachel. 9 Now my mother was Bilhah, daughter of Rotheus the brother of Deborah, Rebecca's nurse, who was born on one and the self-same day with Rachel. 10 And Rotheus was of the family of Abraham, a Chaldean, God-fearing, free-born, and noble 11. And he was taken captive and was bought by Laban ; and he gave him Euna his handmaid to wife, and she bore a daughter, and called her name Zilpah, after the name of the village in which he had been taken captive 12. And next she bore Bilhah, saying My daughter hasteneth after what is new, for immediately that she was born she seized the breast and hastened to suck it

II 1–10   The Constitution of Man

II And I was swift ⌐on my feet⌐ like the deer, and my father Jacob appointed me for all messages, and as a deer did he give me his blessing 2 For as the potter knoweth the vessel, how much it is to contain, and bringeth clay accordingly, so also doth the Lord make the body after the likeness of the spirit, and according to the capacity of the body doth He implant the spirit. 3 And the one doth not fall short of the other by a third part of a hair ; for by weight, and measure, and rule was all the creation made. 4 And as the potter knoweth the use of each vessel, what it is meet for, so also doth the Lord know the body, how far it will persist in goodness, and when it beginneth in evil 5 For there is no inclination or thought which the Lord knoweth not, for He created every man after His own image

6. For as a man's strength, so also is his work ; as

his eye, so also is his sleep; as his soul, so also is his
word either in the law of the Lord or in the law of
Beliar.

7. And as there is a division between light and
darkness, between seeing and hearing, so also is there
a division between man and man, and between woman
and woman; and it is not to be said that the one is
like the other either in face or in mind. 8 ⌈For⌉
God made all things good in their order, the five
senses in the head, and He joined on the neck to the
head, adding to it the hair also for comeliness and
glory, then the heart for understanding, the belly for
excrement, and the stomach for grinding, the wind-
pipe for taking in (the breath), the liver for wrath,
the gall for bitterness, the spleen for laughter, the
reins ⌈for prudence, the muscles of the loins⌉ for
power, the lungs for drawing in, the loins for strength,
and so forth. 9. So ⌈then⌉, my children, let all
your works be done in order with good intent in the
fear of God, and do nothing disorderly in scorn or out
of its due season. 10. For if thou bid the eye to
hear, it cannot; so neither while ye are in darkness
can ye do the works of light.

III. 1-5. An Exhortation to do the Will of God

III. Be ye, therefore, not eager to corrupt your
doings through covetousness or with vain words to
beguile your souls, because if ye keep silence in
purity of heart, ye shall understand how to hold fast
the will of God, and to cast away the will of Beliar.
2. Sun and moon and stars change not their order;
so do ye also change not the law of God in the dis-
orderliness of your doings. 3. The Gentiles went
astray, and forsook the Lord, and changed their
order, and obeyed stocks and stones, spirits of deceit.
4 But ye shall not be so, my children, recognising
in the firmament, in the earth, and in the sea, and in
all created things, the Lord Who made all things, that
ye become not as Sodom, which changed the order of
nature. 5. In like manner the Watchers also changed

the order of their nature, whom the Lord cursed at
the flood, on whose account He made the earth without inhabitant and fruitless

IV. 1-5. Naphtali's Prophecy concerning his Posterity

IV. These things I say unto you, my children, for I
have read in the writing of Enoch that ye yourselves
also shall depart from the Lord, walking according
to all the lawlessness of the Gentiles, and ye shall do
according to all the wickedness of Sodom   2. And
the Lord shall bring captivity upon you, and ⌐there⌐
shall ye serve your enemies, and ye shall be bowed
down with every affliction and tribulation, until the
Lord have consumed you all.   3. And after ye have
become minished and made few, ye shall return and
acknowledge the Lord your God; and He shall bring
you back into your own land, according to His
abundant mercy   4 And it shall be, that after that
they come into the land of their fathers, they shall
again forget the Lord and become ungodly.   5 And
the Lord shall scatter them upon the face of all the
earth, until the compassion of the Lord shall come, a
man working righteousness and working mercy unto
all them that are afar off, and to them that are near.

V. 1–VII. 4. Naphtali's Visions

V For in the fortieth year of my life, I saw a
vision on the Mount of Olives, on the east of Jerusalem, that the sun and the moon were standing still.
2. And behold Isaac, the father of my father, said to
us   Run and lay hold of them, each one according
to his strength, ⌐and to him that seizeth them will
the sun and moon belong⌐   3 And we all of us ran
together, and Levi laid hold of the sun, and Judah
outstripped the others and seized the moon, and they
were both of them lifted up with them. 4. And
when Levi became as a sun, ⌐lo⌐, a certain young man
gave to him twelve branches of palm ; and Judah was
bright as the moon, and under their feet were twelve

rays. [5. And the two, Levi and Judah, ran, and laid hold of them.] 6. And lo, a bull upon the earth, with two great horns, and an eagle's wings upon his back; and we wished to seize him, but could not. 7. But Joseph came, and seized him, and ascended up with him on high. 8. And I saw, for I was there, and behold a holy writing appeared to us, saying: Assyrians, Medes, Persians, [Chaldeans,] Syrians, shall possess in captivity the twelve tribes of Israel.

VI. And again, after seven days, I saw our father Jacob standing by the sea of Jamnia, and we were with him. 2. And, behold, there came a ship sailing by, without sailors or pilot; and there was written upon the ship, The ship of Jacob. 3. And our father saith to us: Come let us embark on our ship. 4. And when we had gone on board, there arose a vehement storm, and a mighty tempest of wind; and our father, who was holding the helm, departed from us. 5. And we, being tost with the tempest, were borne along over the sea; and the ship was filled with water, (and was) pounded by mighty waves, until it was broken up. 6. And Joseph fled away upon a little boat, ⌈and we all were divided upon nine planks,⌉ and Levi and Judah were together. 7. And we were all scattered unto the ends of the earth. 8. Then Levi, girt about with sackcloth, prayed for us all unto the Lord. 9. And when the storm ceased, the ship reached the land, ⌈as it were⌉ in peace. 9. And, lo, our father came, and we all rejoiced with one accord.

VII. These two dreams I told to my father; and he said to me: These things must be fulfilled in their season, after that Israel hath endured many things.

2. Then my father saith unto me: I believe God that Joseph liveth, for I see ⌈always⌉ that the Lord numbereth him with you. 3. And he said, weeping: Ah me, my son, Joseph, thou livest, though I behold thee not, and thou seest not Jacob that begat thee. 4 He caused me also, therefore, to weep by these words, and I burned in my heart to declare that ⌈Joseph⌉ had been sold, but I feared my brethren.

VIII 1-10. **The Last Times. Naphtali's Charge to his Sons**

VIII. And lo ! my children, I have shown unto you the last times, how everything shall come to pass in Israel 2. Do ye also, ⌐therefore,¬ charge your children that they be united to Levi and to Judah ;

For through them shall salvation arise unto Israel,
And in them shall Jacob be blessed.

3 ⌐For through their tribes shall God appear [dwelling among men] on earth,
To save the race of Israel,
And to gather together the righteous from amongst the Gentiles

4 If ye work that which is good, my children,
⌐Both¬ men and angels shall bless you ;
And God shall be glorified among the Gentiles through you,
And the devil shall flee from you,
⌐And the wild beasts shall fear you,¬
And the Lord shall love you,
[And the angels shall cleave to you].

5 As a man who has trained a child well is kept in kindly remembrance ;
So also for a good work there is a good remembrance before God.

6 But him who doeth not that which is good,
⌐Both¬ angels and men shall curse,
And God shall be dishonoured among the Gentiles through him,
And the devil shall make him as his own peculiar instrument,
And every wild beast shall master him,
And the Lord shall hate him.

7. For the commandments of the law are twofold,
⌐And¬ through prudence must they be fulfilled

8 For there is a season for a man to embrace his wife,
And a season to abstain therefrom for his prayer

F

9. So, then, there are two commandments, and, unless they be done in due order, they bring ⌐very great⌐ sin ⌐upon men⌐. So also is it with the other commandments. 10 Be ye therefore wise in God, ⌐my children,⌐ and prudent, understanding the order of His commandments, and the laws of every word, that the Lord may love you.

IX. 1–3. Naphtali's Death and Burial

IX. And when he had charged them with many such words, he exhorted them that they should remove his bones to Hebron, and that they should bury him with his fathers. 2. And when he had eaten and drunken with a merry heart, he covered his face and died 3. And his sons did according to all that Naphtali their father had commanded them.

THE TESTAMENT OF GAD, THE NINTH SON OF JACOB AND ZILPAH

I. 1–II. 5. Introduction. Gad's Hatred of Joseph aforetime

I. THE copy of the testament of Gad, what things he spake unto his sons, in the hundred and twenty-fifth year of his life, saying unto them . 2. ⌐Hearken, my children,⌐ I was the ninth son born to Jacob, and I was valiant in keeping the flocks. 3. Accordingly I guarded ⌐at night⌐ the flock; and whenever the lion came, ⌐or the wolf,⌐ or any wild beast against the fold, I pursued it, and ⌐overtaking (it)⌐ I seized its foot with my hand and hurled it about a stone's throw, and so killed it. 4. Now Joseph ⌐my brother⌐ was feeding the flock with us for upwards of thirty days, and being young, he fell sick by reason of the heat. 5. And he returned to Hebron to our father, who made him lie down near him, because he loved

him greatly   6 And Joseph told our father that the
sons of ⌐Zilpah and⌐ Bilhah were slaying the best
⌐of the flock⌐ and eating them against the judgement
of Reuben and Judah.   7 For he saw that I had
delivered a lamb out of the mouth of the bear, and
put the bear to death ; but had slain the lamb, being
grieved concerning it that it could not live, and that
we had eaten it   8 And regarding this matter I
was wroth with Joseph ⌐until the day that he was
sold   9 And the spirit of hatred was in me,⌐ and
I wished not either to hear of Joseph with the ears,
or to see him with the eyes, because he rebuked us to
our faces ⌐saying⌐ that we were eating of the flock
without Judah   For whatsoever things he told our
father, he believed him

II. I confess now my sin, my children, that often-
times I wished to kill him, because I hated him from
my heart   2 Moreover, I hated him yet more for
his dreams , and I wished to lick him out of the land
of the living, even as an ox licketh up the grass of the
field

3. And Judah sold him secretly to the Ishmaelites.

4 And thus through covetousness we were bent
on slaying him

5. Thus the God of our fathers delivered him from
our hands, that we should not work great lawlessness
in Israel.

III 1-V 11   Gad warns his Sons against Hatred

III And now, my children, hearken to the words
of truth to work righteousness, and all the law of the
Most High, and go not astray through the spirit of
hatred, for it is evil in all the doings of men.   2. Whatsoever a man doeth the hater abominateth him   and
though a man worketh the law of the Lord, he praiseth
him not , though a man feareth the Lord, and taketh
pleasure in that which is righteous, he loveth him
not   3 He dispraiseth the truth, he envieth him
that prospereth, he welcometh evil-speaking, he loveth

arrogance, for hatred blindeth his soul; as I also ⌜then⌝ looked on Joseph.

IV. Beware, therefore, my children, of hatred; for it worketh lawlessness ⌜even⌝ against the Lord Himself. 2. For it will not hear ⌜the words of⌝ His commandments concerning the loving of one's neighbour, ⌜and⌝ it sinneth against God. 3. ⌜For if a brother stumble,⌝ it delighteth immediately to proclaim it to all men, and is urgent that he should be judged for it, and be punished and be put to death. 4. And if it be a servant it stirs him up against his master, and with every affliction it deviseth against him, if possibly he can be put to death. 5 For hatred worketh with envy also against them that prosper : so long as it heareth of or seeth their success, it always languisheth.

6 For as love would quicken ⌜even⌝ the dead, and would call back them that are condemned to die, so hatred would slay the living, and those that had sinned venially it would not suffer to live. 7. For the spirit of hatred worketh together with Satan, through hastiness of spirit, in all things unto men's death; but the spirit of love worketh together with the law of God in long-suffering unto the salvation of men.

V. ⌜Hatred, therefore, is evil,⌝ for it constantly mateth with lying, speaking against the truth; and it maketh small things to be great, and causeth the light to be darkness, and calleth the sweet bitter, and teacheth slander, and ⌜kindleth⌝ wrath, and ⌜stirreth⌝ up war, and violence, and all covetousness; it filleth the heart with evils and devilish poison. 2. These things, ⌜therefore⌝, I say to you from experience, my children, that ye may drive forth hatred, which is of the devil, and cleave to the love of God. 3 Righteousness casteth out hatred, humility destroyeth envy. For he that is just and humble is ashamed to do what is unjust, ⌜being reproved not of another,⌝ but of his own heart, because the Lord looketh on his inclination. 4. He speaketh not against a holy man, because the

fear of God overcometh hatred 5 For fearing lest
he should offend the Lord, he will not do wrong to
any man, even in thought 6 These things I learnt
at last, after I had repented concerning Joseph.
7 For true repentance after a godly sort [destroyeth
ignorance, and] driveth away the darkness, and
enlighteneth the eyes, and giveth knowledge to the
soul, and leadeth the mind to salvation 8 And those
things which it hath not learnt from man, it knoweth
through repentance. 9 For God brought upon me a
disease of the liver; and had not the prayers of
Jacob my father succoured me, it had hardly failed
but my spirit had departed. 10 For by what things
a man transgresseth, by the same also is he punished
11 Since, ⌐therefore,¬ my liver was set mercilessly
against Joseph, in my liver too I suffered mercilessly,
and was judged for eleven months, for so long a time
as I had been angry against Joseph

VI. 1–VIII. 2. Gad exhorts his Sons to love, and to avoid Envy

VI. And now, my children, ⌐I exhort you,¬ love
ye each one his brother, and put away hatred from
your hearts, love one another in deed, and in word, and
in the inclination of the soul 2 For in the presence
of my father I spake peaceably to Joseph ; and when
I had gone out, the spirit of hatred darkened my mind,
and stirred up my soul to slay him. 3. Love ye one
another from the heart, and if a man sin against
thee, speak peaceably to him, and in thy soul hold not
guile ; and if he repent and confess, forgive him 4 But
if he deny it, do not get into a passion with him,
lest catching the poison from thee he take to swearing
and so thou sin doubly. [5. Let not another man
hear thy secrets when engaged in legal strife, lest
he come to hate thee and become thy enemy, and
commit a great sin against thee ; for ofttimes he
addresseth thee guilefully or busieth himself about
thee with wicked intent] 6 And though he deny it
and yet have a sense of shame when reproved, give

over reproving him. For he who denieth may repent so as not to wrong thee again; yea, he may also honour thee, and [fear and] be at peace with thee 7. But if he be shameless and persisteth in his wrongdoing, even so forgive him from the heart, and leave ⌐to God the avenging.

VII. If a man prosper more than you, do not be vexed, but pray also for him,⌐ that he may have perfect prosperity. For so it is expedient for you. 2. And if he be further exalted, be not envious ⌐of him⌐, remembering that all flesh shall die; and offer praise to God, who giveth things good and profitable to all men. 3. Seek out the judgements of the Lord, and thy mind will rest and be at peace. 4. And though a man become rich by evil means, even as Esau, the brother of my father, be not jealous; ⌐but⌐ wait for the end of the Lord. 5. For if He take away (from a man) wealth gotten by evil means He forgiveth him if he repent, but the unrepentant is reserved for eternal punishment 6. For the poor man, if free from envy he pleaseth the Lord in all things, is blessed beyond all men, because he hath not the travail of vain men. 7. Put away, therefore, jealousy from your souls, and love one another with uprightness of heart.

VIII. Do ye also, therefore, tell these things to your children, that they honour Judah and Levi, for from them shall the Lord raise up salvation to Israel. [2. For I know that at the last your children shall depart from Him, and shall walk in all wickedness, and affliction, and corruption before the Lord.]

VIII. 3-5. Gad's Death and Burial

3. And when he had rested for a little while, he said again : My children, obey your father, and bury me near to my fathers. 4. And he drew up his feet, and fell asleep in peace. 5. And after five years they carried him up to Hebron, and laid him with his fathers.

THE TESTAMENT OF ASHER, THE TENTH
SON OF JACOB AND ZILPAH

I 1–VI 6 Asher instructs his Sons concerning
the Good and the Evil Tendency

I THE copy of the testament of Asher, what things
he spake to his sons in the hundred and twenty-fifth
year of his life. 2 ⌐For⌐ while he was still in health,
he said to them Hearken, ye children of Asher, to
your father, and I will declare to you all that is upright in the sight of God 3 Two ways hath God
given to the sons of men, and two inclinations, ⌐and
two kinds of action, and two modes (of action)⌐, and
⌐two⌐ issues 4 Therefore all things are by twos,
one over against the other 5 ⌐For⌐ there are two
ways of good and evil, and with these are the two
inclinations in our breasts discriminating them
6 Therefore if the soul take pleasure in the good.
(inclination), all its actions are in righteousness, and
if it sin it straightway repenteth 7 For, having its
thoughts set upon righteousness, and casting away
wickedness, it straightway overthroweth the evil,
and uprooteth the sin 8 But if it incline to the
evil inclination, all its actions are in wickedness, and
it driveth away the good, and cleaveth to the evil,
and is ruled by Beliar, even though it work what is
good, he perverteth it to evil 9 For whenever it
beginneth to do good, he forceth the issue of the
action into evil for him, seeing that the treasure of
the inclination is filled with an evil spirit.

II A person, then, may with words help the good
for the sake of the evil, yet the issue of the action
leadeth to mischief 2. There is a man who showeth
no compassion upon him who serveth his turn in evil,
and this thing hath two aspects, but the whole is evil.
3 And there is a man that loveth him that worketh
evil, because he would prefer ⌐even⌐ to die in evil
for his sake, and concerning this it is clear that

it hath two aspects, but the whole is an evil work.
4. Though, indeed, he have love, yet is he wicked
who concealeth what is evil for the sake of the good
name, but the end of the action tendeth unto evil.
5. Another stealeth, doeth unjustly, plundereth, defraudeth, and withal pitieth the poor : this ⌜too⌝
hath a twofold aspect, but the whole is evil   6 He
who defraudeth his neighbour provoketh God, and
sweareth falsely against the Most High, and yet
pitieth the poor . the Lord Who commandeth the law
he setteth at nought and provoketh, and yet he
refresheth the poor.   7 He ⌜defileth the soul, and⌝
maketh gay the body ; he killeth many, and pitieth a
few . this, too, hath a twofold aspect, but the whole is
evil.   8 Another committeth adultery and fornication, and abstaineth from meats, and when he fasteth
he doeth evil, and by the power of his wealth over-
whelmeth many ; and notwithstanding his excessive
wickedness he doeth ⌜the⌝ commandments : this, too,
hath a twofold aspect, but the whole is evil.   9. Such
men are hares ; for they are half clean, but in very
deed are unclean   10. For God in the tables of the
commandments hath thus declared.

III. But do not ye, my children, wear two faces
like unto them, of goodness and of wickedness ; but
cleave unto goodness only, for God hath His habita-
tion therein, and men desire it   2 But from wickedness flee away, destroying the (evil) inclination by
your good works ; for they that are double-faced
serve not God, but their own lusts, so that they may
please Beliar and men like unto themselves.

IV. For good men, even they that are of single
face, though they be thought by them that are double-
faced to sin, are just before God   2 For many in
killing the wicked do two works, of good and evil ;
but the whole is good, because he hath uprooted and
destroyed that which is evil.   3. One man hateth
the merciful and unjust man, and the man who committeth adultery and fasteth · this, too, has a twofold aspect, but the ⌜whole⌝ work is good, because

he followeth the Lord's example, in that he accepteth not the seeming good as the genuine good 4. Another desireth not to see a good day with them that riot, lest he defile his body and pollute his soul: this, too, is double-faced, but the whole is good. 5 For such men are like to stags and to hinds, because in the manner of wild animals they seem to be unclean, but they are altogether clean; because ⌈they walk⌉ in zeal for the Lord and abstain from what God also hateth and forbiddeth by His commandments, warding off the evil from the good.

V. Ye see, my children, how that there are two ⌈in all things,⌉ one against the other, and the one is hidden by the other: ⌈in wealth (is hidden) covetousness, in conviviality drunkenness, in laughter grief, in wedlock profligacy⌉ 2 Death succeedeth to life, [dishonour to glory,] night to day, and darkness to light, [and all things are under the day, just things under life, ⌈unjust things under death⌉;] wherefore also eternal life awaiteth death 3 Nor may it be said that truth is a lie, nor right wrong; for all truth is under the light, ⌈even as all things are under God⌉. 4. All these things, therefore, I proved in my life, and I wandered not from the truth of the Lord, and I searched out the commandments of the Most High, walking according to all my strength with singleness of face unto that which is good

VI Take heed, therefore, ye also, my children, to the commandments of the Lord, following the truth with singleness of face 2 For they that are double-faced are guilty of a twofold sin, ⌈for they both do the evil thing and they have pleasure in them that do it,⌉ following the example of the spirits of deceit, and striving against mankind 3. Do ye, ⌈therefore, my children⌉, keep the law of the Lord, and give not heed unto evil as unto good, but look unto the thing that is really good, and keep it in all commandments of the Lord, having your conversation therein, and resting therein 4. For the latter ends of men do show their righteousness (or unrighteousness) when they meet the angels of the Lord and of Satan. 5. For when the soul departeth troubled, it is tormented by the evil spirit which also it served in lusts and evil works. 6. But if he is peaceful with joy he meeteth the angel of peace, and he leadeth him into eternal life

VII. 1–7. Asher's Prophecy concerning his Posterity

VII Become not, my children, as Sodom, which knew not the angels of the Lord, and perished for ever. 2 For I know that ye shall sin, and be delivered into the hands of your enemies, ⌐and⌐ your land shall be made desolate, and your holy places destroyed, and ye shall be scattered unto the four corners of the earth. And ye shall be set at nought in the Dispersion as useless water, 3 Until the Most High shall visit the earth, coming Himself [as man, with men eating and drinking], and breaking the head of the dragon in the water. He shall save Israel and all the Gentiles [God speaking in the person of man] [4 Therefore do ⌐ye also, my children,⌐ tell these things to your children, that they disobey Him not. 5 For I have known that ye shall assuredly be disobedient, and assuredly act ungodly, not giving heed to the law of God, but to the commandments of men, being corrupted through wickedness 6 And therefore shall ye be scattered as Gad and Dan my brethren, and ye shall know not your own lands, tribe, and tongue 7 But the Lord will gather you together in faith through His tender mercy, ⌐and⌐ for the sake of Abraham, Isaac, and Jacob.]

VIII. 1–2. Asher's Death and Burial

VIII And when he had said these things unto them, he commanded saying Bury me in Hebron. And he fell asleep and died at a good old age 2 And his sons did as he had commanded them, and they carried him up to Hebron, and buried him with his fathers.

THE TESTAMENT OF JOSEPH, THE ELEVENTH
SON OF JACOB AND RACHEL

I 1–XVI. 6. Joseph tells the Story of his Life

I THE copy of the testament of Joseph. When he was about to die he called his sons and his brethren together, and said to them : 2 My brethren and my children,

Hearken to Joseph the beloved of Israel ;
Give ear, my sons, unto your father.

3. I have seen in my life envy and death,
Yet I went not astray, ⸢but persevered⸣ in the truth of the Lord.

4. These my brethren hated me, but the Lord loved me :
They wished to slay me, but the God of my fathers guarded me ·
They let me down into a pit, and the Most High brought me up again.

5 I was sold into slavery, and the Lord of all made me free :
I was taken into captivity, and His strong hand succoured me :
I was beset with hunger, and the Lord Himself nourished me.

6. I was alone, and God comforted me :
I was sick, and the Lord visited me :
I was in prison, and my God showed favour unto me ;
In bonds, and He released me ;

7. Slandered, and He pleaded my cause ;
Bitterly spoken against by the Egyptians, and He delivered me ,
Envied by my fellow-slaves, and He exalted me.

II And this chief captain of Pharaoh entrusted to me his house 2 And I struggled against a shameless woman, urging me to transgress with her ; but the God of Israel my father delivered me from the burning flame. 3. I was cast into prison, I was beaten, ⌐I was mocked⌐, but the Lord granted me to find mercy in the sight of the keeper of the prison.

4. For the Lord doth not forsake them that fear Him.
    Neither in darkness, nor in bonds, nor in tribulations, nor in necessities
5. For God is not put to shame as a man,
    Nor as the son of man is He afraid,
    Nor as one that is earth-born is He [weak or] affrighted.
6. But in all these things doth He give protection,
    And in divers ways doth He comfort,
    (Though) for a little space He departeth to try the inclination of the soul
7 In ten temptations He showed me approved,
    And in all of them I endured;
    For endurance is a mighty charm,
    And patience giveth many good things.

III. How often did the Egyptian woman threaten me with death! How often did she give me over to punishment, and then call me back and threaten me, and when I was unwilling to company with her, she said to me : 2. Thou shalt be lord of me, and all that is in mine house, if thou wilt give thyself unto me, and thou shalt be as our master. 3 But I remembered the words of my father, and going into my chamber, I wept and prayed unto the Lord. 4. And I fasted in those seven years, and I appeared to the Egyptians as one living delicately, for they that fast for God's sake receive beauty of face. 5 And if my lord were away from home, I drank no wine, nor for three days did I take my food, but I gave it to the poor and sick. 6. And I sought the Lord early, and I wept for the Egyptian woman of Memphis, for very unceasingly did she trouble me, for also at night she came to me under pretence of visiting me. 7. And because she had no male child she pretended to regard me as a son. 8. And for a time she embraced me as a son, and I knew it not, but later, she sought to draw me into fornication. 9. And when I perceived it I sorrowed unto death; and when she had gone out, I came to myself, and I lamented for her many days, because I recognised her guile and her deceit 10 And I declared unto her the words of the Most High, if haply she would turn from her evil lust

IV. Often, therefore, did she flatter me with words as a holy man, and guilefully in her talk praise my chastity before her husband, while desiring to ensnare me when we were alone 2 ⌜For⌝ she lauded me openly as chaste, and in secret she said unto me Fear not my husband, for he is persuaded concerning thy chastity: for even should one tell him concerning us, he would not believe. 3 Owing to all these things I lay upon the ground, and besought God that the Lord would deliver me from her deceit 4 And when she prevailed nothing ⌜thereby⌝, she came ⌜again⌝ to me under the plea of instruction, that she might learn the word of God 5 And she said unto me If thou willest that I should leave my idols, lie with me, and I will persuade my husband to depart from his idols, and we will walk in the law of thy Lord. 6. And I said unto her The Lord willeth not that those that reverence Him should be in uncleanness, nor doth He take pleasure in them that commit adultery, ⌜but in those that approach Him with a pure heart and undefiled lips⌝ 7 But she held her peace, longing to accomplish her evil desire. 8 And I gave myself yet more to fasting and prayer, that the Lord might deliver me from her

V. ⌜And⌝ again, at another time she said unto me If thou wilt not commit adultery, I will kill my husband by poison, and take thee to be my husband. 2 I therefore, when I heard this, rent my garments, and said unto her Woman, reverence God, and do not this evil deed, lest thou be destroyed; for know indeed that I will declare this thy device unto all men. 3. She therefore, being afraid, besought that

I would not declare this device. 4. And she departed, soothing me with gifts, and sending to me every delight of the sons of men.

VI. And ⌜afterwards⌝ she sent me food mingled with enchantments. 2. And when the eunuch who brought it came, I looked up and beheld a terrible man giving me with the dish a sword, and I perceived that (her) scheme was to beguile me. 3. And ⌜when he had gone out⌝ I wept, nor did I taste that nor any other of her food. 4. So then after one day she came to me and observed the food, and said unto me : Why is it that thou hast not eaten of the food? 5. And I said unto her : It is because thou hast filled it with ⌜deadly⌝ enchantments ; and how saidst thou : I come not near to idols, but to the Lord ⌜alone⌝? 6. Now therefore know that the God of my father hath revealed unto me by His angel thy wickedness, and I have kept it to convict thee, if haply thou mayest see and repent. 7. But that thou mayest learn that the wickedness of the ungodly hath no power over them that worship God with chastity, behold I will take of it and eat before thee. And having so said, I prayed thus : The God of my fathers and the angel of Abraham, be with me, and ate. 8. And ⌜when she saw this⌝ she fell upon her face at my feet, weeping; and I raised her up and admonished her 9. And she promised to do this iniquity no more.

VII. But her heart was still set upon evil, and she looked around how to ensnare me, and sighing deeply she became downcast, though she was not sick. 2. And when her husband saw her, he said unto her : Why is thy countenance fallen? And she said ⌜unto him⌝ : I have a pain at my heart, and the groanings of my spirit oppress me ; and so he comforted her who was not sick. 3. Then accordingly seizing an opportunity she rushed unto me while her husband was yet without, and said unto me : I will hang myself, or cast myself over a cliff, if thou wilt not lie with me. 4. And when I saw the spirit of Beliar was troubling her, I prayed unto the Lord,

and said unto her   5 Why, ⌐wretched woman,⌐ art
thou troubled and disturbed, blinded through sins?
Remember that if thou kill thyself, Asteho, the concu-
bine of thy husband, thy rival, will beat thy children,
and thou wilt destroy thy memorial from off the
earth   6 And she said unto me   Lo, then thou
lovest me, let this suffice me · only strive for my
life ⌐and my children⌐, and I expect that I shall
enjoy my desire ⌐also⌐   7 But she knew not that
because of my lord I spake thus, and not because of
her   8 For if a man hath fallen before the passion
of a wicked desire and become enslaved by it, even
as she, whatever good thing he may hear with regard
to that passion, he receiveth it with a view to his
wicked desire.

VIII   I declare, therefore, unto you, my children,
that it was about the sixth hour when she departed
from me ; and I knelt before the Lord all the day, and
all the night , and about dawn I rose up, weeping the
while and praying for a release from her   2 At
last, then, she laid hold of my garments, forcibly
dragging me to have connection with her   3 When,
⌐therefore,⌐ I saw that in her madness she was holding fast to my garment, I left it behind, and fled
away naked.   4 And holding fast to the garment she
falsely accused me, and when her husband came he
cast me into prison in his house ; and on the morrow
he scourged me and sent me into Pharaoh's prison.
5 And when I was in bonds, the Egyptian woman
was oppressed with grief, and she came and heard
how I gave thanks unto the Lord and sang praises
in the abode of darkness, and with glad voice rejoiced,
glorifying my God that I was delivered from the
lustful desire of the Egyptian woman

IX   And often hath she sent unto me saying : Con-
sent ⌐to fulfil my desire⌐, and I will release thee from
thy bonds, ⌐and I will free thee from the darkness.
2. And not even in thought did I incline unto her
For God loveth him who in a den of darkness combineth fasting with chastity, rather than the man who

in kings' chambers combineth luxury with licence. 3.
And if a man liveth in chastity, and desireth also glory,
and the Most High knoweth that it is expedient for
him, He bestoweth this also upon him, even as upon
me. 4. How often,⌐ though she were sick, did she
come down ⌐to me⌐ at unlooked-for times, and listened
to my voice as I prayed ! And when I heard her
groanings I held my peace. 5. ⌐For⌐ when I was in
her house she was wont to bare her arms, and
breasts, and legs, ⌐that I might lie with her; for she
was⌐ very beautiful, ⌐splendidly adorned⌐ in order
to beguile me. And the Lord guarded me from her
devices.

X. Ye see, therefore, my children, how great
things patience worketh, and prayer with fasting.
2. So ye too, ⌐if ye follow after chastity and purity
with patience and prayer with fasting in humility of
heart, the Lord will dwell among you, because He
loveth chastity 3. And wheresoever the Most High
dwelleth, even though envy, or slavery, or slander
befalleth (a man), the Lord who dwelleth in him, for
the sake of his chastity not only⌐ delivereth him
from evil, ⌐but also exalteth him even as me. 4. For
in every way the man⌐ is lifted up, whether in deed,
or in word, or in thought. 5. My brethren knew how
my father loved me, and yet I did not exalt myself
⌐in my mind⌐ : although I was a child, ⌐I had the fear
of God in my heart⌐ ; for I knew that all things would
pass away. 6. And I did not raise myself (against
them) with evil intent, but I honoured my brethren ;
and out of respect for them, even when I was being
sold, I refrained from telling the Ishmaelites that I
was the son of Jacob, a great man and a mighty.

XI. Do ye also, therefore, my children, ⌐have the
fear of God in all your works before your eyes, and⌐
honour your brethren For every one who doeth
the law of the Lord shall be loved by Him. 2. And
when I came to the Indocolpitæ with the Ishmaelites,
they asked me, saying : Art thou a slave? And I
said that I was a home-born slave, that I might not

put my brethren to shame 3 And the eldest of
them said unto me . Thou art not a slave, for even
thy appearance doth make it manifest But I said
that I was ⌐their⌐ slave 4 Now when we came into
Egypt they strove concerning me, which of them
should buy me and take me 5 Therefore it seemed
good to all that I should remain in Egypt with the
merchant of their trade, until they should return
bringing merchandise 6. And the Lord gave me
favour in the eyes of the merchant, and he entrusted
unto me his house 7. And God blessed him by
my means, and increased him in gold and silver ⌐and
in household servants⌐. 8 And I was with him
three months and five days

XII And about that time the Memphian woman,
the wife of Pentephris, came down ⌐in a chariot⌐,
⌐with great pomp, because she had heard from her
eunuchs concerning me⌐. 2 And she told her
husband that the merchant had become rich by means
of a young Hebrew, and they say that he had assuredly
been stolen out of the land of Canaan 3 Now,
therefore, render justice unto him, and take away the
youth to thy house , so shall the God of the Hebrews
bless thee, for grace from heaven is upon him.

XIII. And Pentephris was persuaded by her words,
and commanded the merchant to be brought, and
said unto him : What is this that I hear ⌐concerning
thee⌐, that thou stealest persons out of the land of
Canaan, and sellest them for slaves ? 2 But the
merchant fell at his feet, and besought him, saying
I beseech thee, my lord, I know not what thou
sayest. 3 And Pentephris said unto him Whence,
then, is the Hebrew slave ? And he said · The
Ishmaelites entrusted him to me until they should
return. 4. But he believed him not, but commanded
him to be stripped and beaten And when he per-
sisted in this statement, Pentephris said Let the
youth be brought. 5 And when I was brought in, I
did obeisance to Pentephris (for he was third in
rank of the officers of Pharaoh) 6 And he took

G

me apart from him, and said unto me : Art thou a slave or free? And I said. A slave. 7. And he said : Whose? And I said : The Ishmaelites'. 8. And he said : How didst thou become their slave? And I said : They bought me out of the land of Canaan. 9. And he said unto me : ⌐Truly⌐ thou liest; and ⌐straightway⌐ he commanded me to be stripped and beaten.

XIV. Now the Memphian woman was looking through a window ⌐at me while I was being beaten, for her house was near, and she sent unto him, saying⌐ : Thy judgement is unjust; for thou dost punish a ⌐free⌐ man who hath been stolen, as though he were a transgressor. 2. And when I made no change in my statement, ⌐though I was beaten,⌐ he ordered me to be imprisoned, until, he said, the owners of the boy should come. 3. And the woman said unto her husband : Wherefore dost thou detain the captive and well-born lad in bonds, who ought rather to be set at liberty, and be waited upon? 4. For she wished to see me out of a desire ⌐of sin⌐, but I was ignorant concerning all these things. 5 And he said to her : It is not the custom of the Egyptians to take away that which belongeth to others before proof is given. 6. This, therefore, he said concerning the merchant; but as for the lad, he must be imprisoned.

XV. Now after four and twenty days came the Ishmaelites; for they had heard that Jacob ⌐my father⌐ was mourning ⌐much⌐ concerning me. And they came and said unto me : 2 How is it that thou saidst that thou wast a slave? and lo, we have learnt that thou art the son of a mighty man in the land of Canaan, and thy father ⌐still⌐ mourneth for thee in sackcloth ⌐and ashes⌐. 3. ⌐When I heard this my bowels were dissolved and my heart melted⌐, and I desired greatly to weep, but I restrained myself, that I should not put my brethren to shame. ⌐And I said unto them, I know not, I am a slave⌐. 4. Then, ⌐therefore⌐, they took counsel to sell me, that I should not be found in their hands. 5 For they feared my father, lest he ⌜should come and⌝ execute upon them a grievous vengeance. For they had heard that he was mighty with God and with men. 6. Then said the merchant unto them Release me from the judgement of Pentephris. 7. And they came and requested me, saying ⌜Say⌝ that thou wast bought by us with money, and he will set us free.

XVI Now the Memphian woman said to her husband Buy the youth; for I hear, said she, that they are selling him   2. And straightway she sent a eunuch to the Ishmaelites, and asked them to sell me 3 But since the eunuch would not agree to buy me (at their price) he returned, having made trial of them, and he made known to his mistress that they asked a large price for their slave. 4. ⌜And she sent another eunuch,⌝ saying Even though they demand two minæ, ⌜give them,⌝ do not spare the gold; only buy the boy, and bring him to me. 5 The eunuch therefore went and gave them eighty pieces of gold, and he received me, but to the Egyptian woman he said : I have given a hundred

6. And though I knew (this) I held my peace, lest the eunuch should be put to shame.

XVII. 1–XVIII 4   Joseph's Exhortation to his Sons

XVII Ye see, therefore, my children, what great things I endured that I should not put my brethren to shame. 2 Do ye also, ⌜therefore,⌝ love one another, ⌜and with long-suffering hide ye one another's faults⌝. 3 For God delighteth ⌜in the unity of brethren, and⌝ in the purpose of a heart that taketh pleasure in love 4 And when my brethren came into Egypt they learnt that I had returned their money unto them, and upbraided them not, and comforted them. 5 And after the death of Jacob my father I loved them ⌜more abundantly⌝, and all things whatsoever he commanded I did ⌜very abundantly⌝ for them 6. And I suffered them not to be afflicted even in the smallest matter; and all that was in my hand I gave unto them. 7. ⌐And¬ their children were my children, and my children as their servants; and their life was my life, and all their suffering was my suffering, ⌐and all their sickness was my infirmity¬. My land was their land, and their counsel my counsel. 8. And I exalted not myself among them ⌐in arrogance¬ because of my ⌐worldly¬ glory, ⌐but I was among them as one of the least¬.

XVIII. If ye also, therefore, walk in the commandments of the Lord, my children, He will exalt you there, and will bless you with good things for ever and ever. 2. ⌐And if any one seeketh to do evil unto you, do well unto him, and pray for him, and ye shall be redeemed of the Lord from all evil.¬ 3. ⌐For,¬ behold, ye see that ⌐out of my humility and long-suffering¬ I took unto wife the daughter of the priest of Heliopolis. And a hundred talents of gold were given me with her, and the Lord made them to serve me. 4. And He gave me also beauty as a flower beyond the beautiful ones of Israel; and He preserved me ⌐unto old age in strength and¬ in beauty, because I was like in all things to Jacob.

XIX. 1-12. Joseph's Vision (from the Armenian Version).

XIX. Hear ye, therefore, the vision which I saw. 2. I saw twelve harts feeding. And nine of them were dispersed. Now the three were preserved, but on the following day they also were dispersed. 3. And I saw that the three harts became three lambs, and they cried to the Lord, and He brought them forth into a flourishing and well-watered place, yea He brought them out of darkness into light. 4. And there they cried unto the Lord until there gathered together to them the nine harts, and they became as twelve sheep, and after a little time they increased and became many flocks. 5. And after these things I saw and behold, twelve bulls were sucking one cow, which produced a sea of milk, and there drank thereof the twelve flocks and innumerable herds 6. And the horns of the fourth bull went up unto heaven and became as a wall for the flocks, and in the midst of the [two] horns there grew another horn. 7. And I saw a bull calf which surrounded them twelve times, and it became a help to the bulls wholly 8 And I saw in the midst of the horns a virgin [wearing a many-coloured garment, and from her] went forth a lamb, and on his right (was as it were a lion; and) all the beasts and all the reptiles rushed (against him), and the lamb overcame them and destroyed them. 9 And the bulls rejoiced because of him, and the cow [and the harts] exulted together with them 10. And these things must come to pass in their season 11 And do ye, my children, honour Levi and Judah, for from them shall arise the salvation of Israel. 12 For my kingdom which is among you shall come to an end as a watcher's hammock, which will not appear after the summer

XX. 1-6. Joseph's Last Words to his Sons. His Death and Burial

XX ⌜For⌝ I know that after my death the Egyptians will afflict you, but God will avenge you, and will bring you into that which He promised to your fathers 2. But ye shall carry up my bones with you; ⌜for when my bones are being taken up thither, the Lord shall be with you in light, and Beliar shall be in darkness with the Egyptians⌝ 3 And carry ye up Asenath your mother [to the Hippodrome], and near Rachel your mother bury her 4 And when he had said these things he stretched out his feet, and died at a good old age. 5 And all Israel mourned for him, and all Egypt, with a great mourning 6 And when the children of Israel went out of Egypt, they took with them the bones of Joseph, and they buried him in Hebron with his fathers, and the years of his life were one hundred and ten years

THE TESTAMENT OF BENJAMIN,
THE TWELFTH SON OF JACOB AND RACHEL

I. 1–6. Introduction. Benjamin's Birth

I. THE copy of the words of Benjamin, which he commanded his sons to observe, after he had lived a hundred and twenty-five years. 2. And he kissed them, and said : As Isaac was born to Abraham in his old age, so also was I to Jacob. 3. And since Rachel my mother died in giving me birth, I had no milk, therefore I was suckled by Bilhah her handmaid. 4 For Rachel remained barren for twelve years ⌐after she had borne Joseph⌐; and she prayed the Lord ⌐with fasting twelve days, and she conceived and bare me⌐. 5. For ⌐my father⌐ loved Rachel dearly, ⌐and prayed that he might see two sons born from her⌐. 6. Therefore was I called Benjamin, that is, a son of days.

II. 1–5. Benjamin and Joseph in Egypt

II. And when I went into Egypt, to Joseph, and my brother recognised me, he said unto me . What did they tell my father when they sold me ? 2. And I said ⌐unto him⌐, They dabbled thy coat with blood and sent it, and said . Know whether this be thy son's coat ? 3 And he said unto me : Even so, brother, when they had stripped me of my coat they gave me to the Ishmaelites, and they gave me a loin cloth, and scourged me, and bade me run. 4 And as for one of them that had beaten me with a rod, a lion met him and slew him. 5 And so his associates were affrighted

III. 1–V. 5. Benjamin exhorts his Sons to Goodness after the Example of Joseph

III. Do ye also, therefore, my children, ⌐love the Lord God of heaven and earth, and keep His com-

mandments⌐, following the example of the good and
holy man ⌐Joseph⌐. 2. And let your mind be unto
good, even as ye know me; for he that hath his mind
right, seeth all things rightly 3. Fear ye the Lord,
and love your neighbour, and even though the spirits
of Beliar claim you to afflict you with every evil, yet
shall they not have dominion over you, even as they
had not over Joseph my brother 4 How many men
wished to slay him, and God shielded him ! For he
that feareth God and loveth his neighbour cannot be
smitten by the spirit of Beliar, being shielded by the
fear of God 5 Nor can he be ruled over by the
device of men or beasts, for he is helped by the Lord
through the love which he hath towards his neighbour
6. For Joseph also besought our father ⌐that he
would pray for his brethren⌐, that ⌐the Lord⌐ would
not impute to them as sin ⌐whatever evil they had
done unto him ⌐ 7. And thus Jacob cried out :
My good child, thou hast prevailed over the bowels
of thy father Jacob And he embraced him, and
kissed him for two hours, saying 8 In thee shall be
fulfilled the prophecy of heaven [concerning the Lamb
of God, and Saviour of the world], that a blameless
one shall be delivered up for lawless men, and a sinless
shall die for ungodly men [in the blood of the coven-
ant, for the salvation of the Gentiles and of Israel,
and shall destroy Beliar and his servants].

IV See ye, therefore, my children, the end of the
good man ? Be followers of his ⌐compassion, therefore, with a good mind⌐, that ⌐ye also⌐ may wear
crowns of glory 2. For the good man hath not a
dark eye ; for he showeth mercy to all men, even
though they be sinners. 3 ⌐And though they devise
with evil intent concerning him, by doing good he
overcometh evil, being shielded by God;⌐ and he
loveth the righteous as his own soul 4 If any one
is glorified, he envieth him not ; if any one is enriched,
he is not jealous, if any one is valiant, he praiseth
him, the virtuous man he laudeth ; ⌐on the poor
man he hath mercy, on the weak he hath compassion ;

unto God he singeth praises⌐. 5. And him that hath
the grace of a good spirit he loveth as his own soul.

V. If, ⌐therefore, ye also⌐ have a good ⌐mind⌐, then
will both wicked men be at peace with you, and the
profligate will reverence you ⌐and turn unto good;
and the covetous will not only cease from their
inordinate desire, but even give the objects of their
covetousness to them that are afflicted. 2. If ye
do well, even the unclean spirits will flee from you⌐;
and the beasts will dread you. 3. ⌐For where there
is reverence for good works and light in the mind,
even darkness fleeth away from him.⌐ 4. ⌐For⌐ if
any one doeth violence to a holy man, he repenteth;
for ⌐the holy man⌐ is merciful to his reviler, and
holdeth his peace. 5. And if any one betrayeth a
righteous man, the righteous man prayeth: though
for a little he be humbled, yet not long after he
appeareth far more glorious, as was Joseph my
brother.

VI. 1–7. The Good Inclination

VI. The inclination of the good man is not in the
power of the deceit of the spirit of Beliar, for the
angel of peace guideth his soul. 2. ⌐And⌐ he gazeth
not ⌐passionately⌐ upon corruptible things, nor
gathereth together riches ⌐through a desire of plea-
sure⌐. 3. He delighteth not in pleasure, ⌐[he grieveth
not his neighbour], he sateth not himself with luxuries,
he erreth not in the uplifting of the eyes⌐, for the Lord
is his portion. 4. The good inclination receiveth not
glory ⌐nor dishonour⌐ from men, and it knoweth not
any guile, or lie, or fighting, or reviling; for the Lord
dwelleth in him and lighteth up his soul, and he
rejoiceth towards all men alway. 5. The good mind
hath not two tongues, of blessing and of cursing, of
contumely and ⌐of honour⌐, of sorrow and of joy, of
quietness and of confusion, of hypocrisy and of truth,
[of poverty and of wealth]; but it hath one ⌐disposi-
tion⌐, uncorrupt and pure, concerning all men. 6. It
hath no double sight, nor double hearing; for in

everything which he doeth, ⌜or speaketh, or seeth, he knoweth that the Lord looketh on his soul. 7. And he cleanseth his mind that he be not condemned by men as well as⌝ by God. And in like manner the works of Beliar are twofold, and there is no singleness in them.

VII. 1–5. The Sword of Beliar ; the Warning of Cain

VII. Therefore, my children, I tell you, flee the malice of Beliar, for he giveth a sword to them that obey him. 2. And the sword is the mother of seven evils First the mind conceiveth through Beliar, and first there is bloodshed, secondly, ruin; thirdly, tribulation; fourthly, exile; fifthly, dearth; sixthly, panic, seventhly, destruction. 3. Therefore was Cain also delivered over to seven vengeances by God, for in every hundred years the Lord brought one plague upon him. 4 And when he was two hundred years old he began to suffer, and in the nine-hundredth year he was destroyed. For on account of Abel, his brother, with all the evils was he judged, but Lamech with seventy times seven. 5. Because forever those who are like unto Cain ⌜in envy and hatred of brethren⌝, shall be punished ⌜with the same judgement⌝.

VIII. 1–3   Benjamin exhorteth his Sons to flee from Evil

VIII. And do ye, my children, flee evil-doing, envy, and hatred of brethren, and cleave to goodness and love 2. He that hath a pure mind in love, looketh not after a woman with a view to fornication; for he hath no defilement in his heart, because the Spirit of God resteth upon him. 3 For ⌜as⌝ the sun is not defiled by shining on dung and mire, ⌜but rather drieth up both and driveth away the evil smell⌝; so also the pure mind, though encompassed by the defilements of earth, rather cleanseth (them), and is not itself defiled.

IX. 1-5. Benjamin's Prophecy concerning his Posterity

IX. And I believe that there will be also evil-doings among you, from the words of Enoch the righteous : that ye shall commit fornication with the fornication of Sodom, and shall perish, all save a few, and shall renew wanton deeds with women ; and the kingdom of the Lord shall not be among you, for straightway He shall take it away. 2. Nevertheless the temple of God shall be in your portion, and the last (temple) shall be more glorious than the first. And the twelve tribes shall be gathered together there, and all the Gentiles, until the Most High shall send forth His salvation in the visitation of an only-begotten prophet. 3. [And He shall enter into the [first] temple, and there shall the Lord be treated with outrage, and He shall be lifted up upon a tree. 4. And the veil of the temple shall be rent, and the Spirit of God shall pass on to the Gentiles as fire poured forth. 5 And He shall ascend from Hades and shall pass from earth into heaven. And I know how lowly He shall be upon earth, and how glorious in heaven.]

X. 1. Benjamin's Vision of Joseph

X. Now when Joseph was in Egypt, I longed to see his figure ⌐and the form of his countenance⌐; and through the prayers of Jacob my father I saw him, while awake in the day-time, even his entire figure exactly as he was.

X. 2-10. Benjamin's Inheritance to his Sons

2. ⌐And when he had said these things, he said unto them :⌐ Know ye, therefore, my children, that I am dying. 3. Do ye, therefore, truth each one to his neighbour, and keep the law of the Lord and His commandments. 4. For these things do I leave you instead of inheritance. Do ye also, ⌐therefore,⌐ give them to your children for an everlasting possession ; for so did both Abraham, and Isaac, and Jacob. 5. For

all these things they gave us for an inheritance,
saying : Keep the commandments of God, until the
Lord shall reveal His salvation to all Gentiles.   6.
┌And┐ then shall ye see Enoch, Noah, and Shem, and
Abraham, and Isaac, and Jacob, rising on the right
hand in gladness   7. Then shall we also rise, each one
over our tribe, worshipping the King of heaven, [Who
appeared upon earth in the form of a man in humility
And as many as believe on Him on the earth shall rejoice with Him].   8. Then also all men shall rise, some
unto glory and some unto shame   And the Lord shall
judge Israel first, for their unrighteousness, [for
when He appeared as God in the flesh to deliver
them they believed Him not]   9 And then shall He
judge all the Gentiles, [as many as believed Him not
when He appeared upon earth]   10 And He shall
convict Israel through the chosen ones of the Gentiles,
even as he reproved Esau through the Madianites,
who deceived their brethren, [so that they fell into
fornication, and idolatry ; and they were alienated
from God,] becoming therefore children in the portion
of them that fear the Lord

X. 11–XI. 5. A further Prophecy concerning Benjamin's Posterity

11. If ye ┌therefore, my children,┐ walk in holiness
┌according to the commandments of the Lord,┐ ye
shall again dwell securely with me, and all Israel shall
be gathered unto the Lord.

XI And I shall no longer be called a ravening
wolf on account of your ravages, but [a worker of the
Lord distributing food to them that work what is
good   2. And there shall arise in the latter days]
one beloved of the Lord, [of the tribe of Judah and
Levi┐, a doer of His good pleasure in his mouth, [with
new knowledge enlightening the Gentiles].   3 Until
the consummation of the age shall he be in the syna-
gogues of the Gentiles, and among their rulers, as a
strain of music in the mouth of all.   4. And he shall be
inscribed in the holy books, both his work and his word,

and he shall be a chosen one of God for ever. 5.
And through them he shall go to and fro as Jacob my
father, saying : He shall fill up that which lacketh of
thy tribe].

XII 1-4   Benjamin's Death and Burial

XII And when he had said these things he stretched
out his feet, 2 And died in [a beautiful] and good
sleep. 3. And his sons did as he had enjoined them,
and they took up his body and buried it in Hebron
with his fathers 4. And the number (of the days)
of his life were a hundred and twenty-five years.

PRINTED IN GREAT BRITAIN BY RICHARD CLAY & SONS, LIMITED,
BRUNSWICK ST., STAMFORD ST , S.E , AND BUNGAY, SUFFOLK.

TRANSLATIONS OF EARLY DOCUMENTS

A Series of texts important for the study of Christian origins, by various authors

UNDER THE JOINT EDITORSHIP OF

The Rev. W. O. E. OESTERLEY, D.D.

AND

The Rev. CANON G H. BOX, M.A.

THE object of the Series is to provide short, cheap, and handy text-books for students, either working by themselves or in classes. The aim is to furnish in translations important texts unencumbered by commentary or elaborate notes, which can be had in larger works.

FIRST SERIES

Palestinian-Jewish and Cognate Texts
(Pre-Rabbinic)

1. Aramaic Papyri. A. E. Cowley, Litt.D., Sub-Librarian of the Bodleian Library, Oxford.

2. The Wisdom of Ben-Sira (Ecclesiasticus). The Rev. W. O. E. Oesterley, D.D., Vicar of St. Alban's, Bedford Park, W.; Examining Chaplain to the Bishop of London.

3. The Book of Enoch. The Rev. R. H. Charles, D.D., Canon of Westminster.

4. The Book of Jubilees. The Rev. Canon Charles.

5. The Testaments of the Twelve Patriarchs. The Rev. Canon Charles.

6. The Odes and Psalms of Solomon. The Rev. G. H. Box, M.A., Rector of Sutton, Beds., Hon. Canon of St. Alban's.

7. The Martyrdom of Isaiah. The Rev. Canon Charles.

8. The Second (Fourth) Book of Ezra. The Rev. Canon Box.

9. The Apocalypse of Baruch. The Rev. Canon Charles.

10. The Assumption of Moses. The Rev. W. J. Ferrar, M.A., Vicar of Holy Trinity, East Finchley.

SECOND SERIES
Hellenistic-Jewish Texts

---

1. The Wisdom of Solomon. The Rev. Dr. Oesterley.

2. The Sibylline Oracles (Books iii–v). The Rev. H. N. Bate, M.A., Vicar of Christ Church, Lancaster Gate, W.; Examining Chaplain to the Bishop of London.

3. The Letter of Aristeas. H. St. John Thackeray, M.A, King's College, Cambridge; Grinfield Lecturer in the Septuagint in the University of Oxford.

4. Selections from Philo. J. H. A. Hart, B.D., Fellow and Lecturer of St. John's College, Cambridge.

5. Selections from Josephus. H. St. John Thackeray, M.A.

6. The Fourth Book of Maccabees. The Rev. C. W. Emmet, M.A., Vicar of West Hendred, Oxon.

THIRD SERIES

Palestinian-Jewish and Cognate Texts (Rabbinic)

———— -- -

*1. Pirqe Aboth. The Rev. Dr. Oesterley.

*2. Berakhoth. The Rev. A. Lukyn Williams, D.D., Vicar of Guilden Morden, Hon. Canon of Ely.

*3. Yoma. The Rev. Canon Box.

*4. Megillath Taanith. The Rev. Canon Box.

————

5. Tamid	11. Megillah
6. Shabbath	12. Sukkah
7. Sanhedrin	13. Taanith
8. Abodah Zara	14. Qimchi's Commentary on the Psalms (Book i)
9. Middoth	
10. Sopherim	

—— — -- --- ———

* It is proposed to publish these texts first by way of experiment. If the Series should so far prove successful the others will follow.

— — . . — - — ——

SOCIETY FOR PROMOTING CHRISTIAN KNOWLEDGE

London. 68, Haymarket, S W ; 43, Queen Victoria Street, E.C
Brighton: 129, North Street

AND ALL BOOKSELLERS

CPSIA information can be obtained
at www.ICGtesting.com
Printed in the USA
BVHW051459090120
569077BV00003B/76/P